» Songs of Love & Grief

» Heinrich Heine

Songs *of* Love *&* Grief

A BILINGUAL ANTHOLOGY TRANSLATED

IN THE VERSE FORMS OF THE ORIGINALS

BY WALTER W. ARNDT

WITH A FOREWORD AND NOTES BY

JEFFREY L. SAMMONS

NORTHWESTERN UNIVERSITY PRESS

EVANSTON, ILLINOIS

Northwestern University Press
Evanston, Illinois 60208-4210
Copyright © 1995 by
Northwestern University Press.
Published 1995
All rights reserved.
Printed in the United States of America
ISBN 0-8101-1323-6 (cloth)
ISBN 0-8101-1324-4 (paper)
Library of Congress
Cataloging-in-Publication Data
Heine, Heinrich, 1797–1856.

    [Poems. English & German. Selections]
    Songs of love and grief : a bilingual anthology
in the verse forms of the originals / Heinrich Heine ;
translated by Walter W. Arndt ; with a foreword
and annotated by Jeffrey L. Sammons.

      p.   cm.—(European poetry classics)
    English and German.
    Includes bibliographical references.
    ISBN 0-8101-1323-6 (alk. paper).—
    ISBN 0-8101-1324-4 (pbk. : alk. paper)
    1. Heine, Heinrich, 1797–1856—Translations
into English. I. Arndt, Walter W., 1916– .
II. Title. III. Series.
PT2316.A4A76 1995
831'.7—dc20   95-36589
                         CIP

The paper used in this publication meets the
minimum requirements of the American National
Standard for Information Sciences—Permanence
of Paper for Printed Library Materials,
ANSI Z39.48-1984.

» Contents

» Contents

Ich stand in dunklen Träumen, 56

Sie liebten sich beide, doch keiner, 58

Und als ich euch meine Schmerzen geklagt, 60

Mensch, verspotte nicht den Teufel, 62

Mein Kind, wir waren Kinder, 64

Im Traum sah ich die Geliebte, 68

Herz, mein Herz, sei nicht beklommen, 70

Du bist wie eine Blume, 72

Kind! es wäre dein Verderben, 74

Ich wollte bei dir weilen, 76

Saphire sind die Augen dein, 78

Zu fragmentarisch ist Welt und Leben!, 80

Ich wollte, meine Schmerzen ergössen, 82

Du hast Diamanten und Perlen, 84

Gaben mir Rat und gute Lehren, 86

Wir fuhren allein im dunkeln, 88

Und bist du erst mein ehlich Weib, 90

Der Tod das ist die kühle Nacht, 92

Zu der Lauheit und der Flauheit, 94

From *Neue Gedichte*

I. NEUER FRÜHLING

Leise zieht durch mein Gemüt, 98

Wenn du mir vorüberwandelst, 100

Mit deinen blauen Augen, 102

Ich wandle unter Blumen, 104

Es haben unsre Herzen, 106

Küsse, die man stiehlt im Dunkeln, 108

Morgens send ich dir die Veilchen, 110

Der Brief, den du geschrieben, 112

Die holden Wünsche blühen, 114

Himmel grau und wochentäglich!, 116

From *New Poems*

I. NEW SPRINGTIME

» Foreword

In October 1827, the Hamburg firm of Hoffmann und Campe brought out a modestly titled *Book of Songs (Buch der Lieder)* by a twenty-nine-year-old unemployed doctor of laws and grudgingly baptized Jew, H. Heine, as he always called himself in public. The proprietor, Julius Campe, had no great expectations and paid nothing for the book at the time; he took it on as a favor to an author he wanted to have. Campe, on his way to becoming the most ingenious and fearless publisher of dissident and radical writing in the oppressed German states, was interested in Heinrich Heine's *Travel Pictures (Reisebilder)*, an original genre amalgamating sentiment and wit, fiction and essay, journalistic chitchat and ironically coded subversion. Nor did Heine, for his part, seem to set great store by the poetry volume. Most of the 240 poems had been published before, some more than once, during the several years preceding. He had a bad conscience about lyrical poetry as an evasive distraction from imperatives of the time that could only be addressed in militantly engaged prose. Neither man could then foresee that the *Book of Songs* would become the most famous book of German poetry in the world, and it was some years before that fame began to be manifest.

In those days Germany was full of verse. Everyone wrote it, from schoolchildren to government ministers, even the king of Bavaria, and, if possible, published it in almanacs, calendars, journals, and newspapers. It had become too easy to write; the ubiquity dulled critical discrimination. Because Heine drew from and recapitulated the images and vocabulary, the motifs and forms of the domesticated late Romanticism derived from the folk song, it took an attentive and carefully tuned ear to apprehend his special qualities at the time. In fact, it was not refined criticism but an inchoate instinctive sensibility in the reading public that gradually lifted his poetry out of the mass production of his contemporaries. Campe's sense of the market was reliable in the short run, as it usually was. The first edition of two thousand copies lasted for a decade; a second edition did not come out until 1837. Then the book began to pick up speed: a third edition appeared in 1839, a fourth in 1841, a fifth in 1844, the last revised by Heine and thus the standard we read today. Eight further editions appeared in his lifetime and innumerable others to the present day. It is no accident that this acceleration accompanied the evolution of the German art song, for Heine's poetry went out into the world, in his own phrase, "on wings of song." The pivotal work, perhaps, Robert Schumann's *Dichterliebe* (Opus 48), dates from 1840. It has been said that no poet other than the biblical psalmist has been set to music more often than Heine. To date some eight thousand settings of his works have been identified. Some of this music makes it difficult to hear Heine's spoken words; it takes almost physical effort to *read* the Lorelei poem after having heard Friedrich Silcher's crooning blare from a loudspeaker as the Rhine boat passes St. Goar.

The *Book of Songs* is divided into sections that are in chronological order, although their contents are not necessarily so, for Heine was a meticulously revising, constantly reshuffling, and recomposing poet. The first section of early poems, *Youthful Sufferings (Junge Leiden)*, is divided into "Dream Images" ("Traumbilder"); "Songs" ("Lieder"); "Romances" ("Romanzen"), one of the terms he used for the narrative ballad poetry he wrote all his life; and "Sonnets" ("Sonette"), an experiment in Romantic form not to be repeated. There follow the two sequences that are the ground of his world fame, with which he began his curious habit of grouping poems in multiples of eleven: the sixty-six poems of *Lyrical Intermezzo (Lyrisches Intermezzo)*, so called because they originally appeared in 1823 between two tragedies today remembered only by specialists, and the eighty-eight poems of *Homecoming (Die Heimkehr)*, mostly composed when he had drifted back to Hamburg after completing his university degree in 1825. Finally there are the two cycles of *The North Sea (Die Nordsee)*, twenty-two poems in all, the product of vacations on the island of Norderney in 1825 and 1826. They are the first major poems of the sea in German literature, composed in expansive, rolling free verse, a mode he did not pursue subsequently, perhaps because he sensed that a certain inborn glibness required the discipline of bound forms.

Overwhelmingly, the poems of the *Book of Songs* are concerned with unrequited love. In German poetry there had not been so obsessive a treatment of this theme since the high Middle Ages. Readers of the past attempted to translate the poetry into biography, associating it with Heine's unsuccessful wooing of his cousin Amalie Heine, and perhaps also of her sister Therese. Much of this romance is a product of imaginative speculation, for he was always extremely reticent about his inner self and personal life, and it has been doubted that these famous love affairs ever occurred at all. Since the poetry does not yield a coherent and plausible record of experience, modern critics came to sever the poems from the life altogether, treating them as formal Petrarchan exercises. It would be more accurate to put them into the anti-Petrarchan tradition, for rarely has there been a body of poetry in which the beloved in all her guises receives such an embittered thrashing:

> You have diamonds, you have pearls,
> You have all that heart may crave;
> You have the most beautiful eyes;
> My love, what more would you have?

The poet yearns to see her punished:

> In a dream I saw the beloved,
> A woman worn and downcast,
> Haggard and raddled the body
> So blooming and fresh in the past.

The suppression of the alleged biographical interest has been of value insofar as it has drawn attention to the art of the poetry. But, in all probability, the biographical link was cut too emphatically. The evidence that Heine in his protracted adolescence fancied himself in love with Amalie and then, for a time, with Therese, is slender but firm. After all, they were both heiresses of his millionaire uncle Salomon Heine, possibly the richest commoner in all of Germany, whose preposterous fortune hypnotized and vexed the needy, demanding nephew for the greater part of his life.

However, the poetry is not a record of these experiences, but of the process of overcoming their shame and humiliation through a display of poetic powers. The poetry and what it is doing for the poet are ultimately the subject of the poetry rather than the beloved or the love story. The poet recovers his shaken dignity through the creative achievement:

> "I am a German poet
> Well-known in the German world;
> Where the foremost names are mentioned,
> My name is also heard."

On the other hand, the poetry may be a poor substitute for real gratification:

> The time I came to you with my plaints,
> You gave me yawns and nothing more;

> But when I cast them in graceful quatrains,
> You paid me compliments galore.

Feeling is broken up and undercut by irony, but, once dismissed as delusion, returns nevertheless as imperishably genuine; a poem not included in this selection ends in the antinomy of real and pretended feeling: "With death in my own heart / I have played the dying swordsman." The poet's relationship to traditional nature imagery remains insecure; he hopes, to be sure, to be able to invoke the pathetic fallacy—"The blossoms gossip and whisper / And watch me regretful and sad"—but the likelihood is that nature is indifferently alien to the imagination:

> Now murmurs the wind in the leafage,
> And the creaking oak limbs seem
> To ask: "Mad horseman, what would you
> With that nonsensical dream?"

Genre pictures are undone: the poet wishes that the sentry, an awkward figure in a charming landscape, would shoot him dead. The exotic can be beautiful: "The Ganges, all blaze and fragrance, / Where blossoming trees loom up"; but also ugly: "In Lappland people are dirty, / Flat-headed, wide-muzzled, small." The tone shifts back and forth from the emotional to the conversational, from the delicate to the blunt; the setting from the realm of dreams and the exotic imagination to the banal scenes of modern society. It is all true: the feeling and the frustration, the hope and the delusion, the desirability of the beloved and her dim-witted cruelty. Recurrently the poems mount a commentary on the poetry itself—"Out of my aching smart / I fashion my little songs"—so that Barker Fairley, a pioneer of modern Heine interpretation, entitled the first section of his study "Song within Song." The fact is that no other poet of his age queried the possibilities and even the permissibility of poetry so persistently and desperately as Heine.

Although the sovereign, powerful persona of a poet, wrenched out of his disappointments and marginality, was crucial to his identity and self-esteem, he tended nevertheless to regard poetry, like love, as a vice, and he repeatedly swore off it in the interest of what he regarded as more urgent purposes in the struggle for progress, enlightenment, and liberty. But the poetry would not remain quiescent; recurrently, he found himself returning to it. In the winter of 1830–31, in response to a commission by a composer, he began to organize what were to be the forty-four poems of *New Spring (Neuer Frühling)*, which recapitulate the tone and motifs of the love poetry of the *Book of Songs* with greater polish and distance. They, too, have often been set to music. They formed the first section of his second book of poetry, *New Poems (Neue Gedichte)*, first published in 1844. The second section, *Variae (Verschiedene)*, consists of a series of cycles depicting short-lived sexual encounters with the blithe women of Paris, where Heine, beginning in 1831, lived in first voluntary, then involuntary, exile. These poems caused much offense, as they were doubtless intended to do, and, again back-translated into biography, generated salacious speculation about his libertine, depraved way of life, much of it very likely imaginary. The poems are often taken to be expressions of liberated sensuality, reflecting Heine's discipleship to the protosocialist and sexually emancipatory Saint-Simonian movement in France, but it has been less noticed that the cycles, though they peak in gaiety and sensual excitement, tend to end with satiety, betrayal, and loss; woman is bitter, and the carnival concludes with Ash Wednesday: "We must have reached our end long since / When we had scarce begun." The flimsy encounters do not, in the long run, fulfill the poet's longings. Heine was enthusiastic about life in Paris but never fully acclimated to France; he remained homesick for Germany, where he was so unwelcome:

> The oak trees are green, and blue are the eyes
> Of German women; they languish a bit,
> They whisper of love and of hope and of faith;
> This I can't stand—there are reasons for it.

And: "I had a handsome homeland long ago . . . I dreamed it all"; see also "Anno 1839."

The third section of *New Poems* is made up of more of his ballads, again titled *Romances (Romanzen)*. The fourth section, *Poems of the Times (Zeitgedichte)*, consists of sardonically slashing political verse. Heine was never fully persuaded that poetry was the appropriate vehicle for political activism, but a number of liberal and radical poets had emerged whose popularity threatened his self-understanding as the most advanced of revolutionaries. Since he regarded them as naive, bourgeois, and infected with German nationalism, he determined to drive them from the field by beating them at their own game. The most important result, appended to *New Poems,* was what may still be regarded as the greatest political poem in the German language, the two thousand–line mock-epic *Germany. A Winter's Tale (Deutschland. Ein Wintermärchen)*, product of a risky journey home in 1843. Our excerpts include the canto in which the traveling poet visits Emperor Barbarossa, emblem of the frustrated yearnings of German nationalism, in his refuge in the Kyffhäuser mountain and catches him up on the revolutionary events of the past century. It should always be remembered, however, that Heine wrote another mock-epic of the same length, begun before the *Winter's Tale* and completed after it: *Atta Troll: A Midsummer Night's Dream (Atta Troll: Ein Sommernachtstraum)*, in which he satirizes uncouth egalitarianism and the clumsiness of the political poets in the figure of a dancing bear.

Almost simultaneously with the ultimately disappointing revolution of 1848, Heine's health gave way. It had been deteriorating with worrisome symptoms for some years, but in the spring of that year he collapsed into paralysis, never to walk again, remaining confined to his "mattress grave" for eight long, wearisome years of pain and suffering. The exact nature of his illness has been disputed to the present day, but the important thing is that he thought it was venereal, and thus it obliged a reconsideration of his investment in sensualist emancipation. He expressed the revision in religious terms, repudiating the belligerent secularism he had long propagated and acknowledging his need for a personal God. An aspect of this change is a resuscitation of his Jewish identity, which he had tried to regard as obsolete but which had been working subliminally in him at least since the late 1830s. That identity emerged to the surface of public commitment on the occasion of a horrific pogrom in Damascus in 1840. Yet he was determined not to appear pious or reactionary; he made it clear that his religious return was born of a need to complain to the highest authority of his relentless sufferings and the unjust governance of the world, and to permit himself blasphemies that would have seemed irrelevant in the fullness of health.

In his pain, isolation, and disappointed hopes, he turned again to the resource that had sustained him in the past: poetry. His third volume of poems, *Romanzero* (1851), gives voice to the cruelty of human relations and the baffling arbitrariness of divine justice, yet articulates resistance in the ingenuity, color, and pungency of the poetry itself. The book is divided into three parts. The first section is called *Histories (Historien),* another term for his narrative romances, a number of them dealing with the tragedies of kings, heroes, and poets, the doomed better men of his late vision of the existential injustice of the world. The second, titled, after Jeremiah, *Lamentations (Lamentationen)*, contains satirical and political verse, but also a group of short poems subtitled "Lazarus," named after the miserable pauper in the Gospel of Luke, in which the poet's suffering generates hard questions about God's apparent indifference to the evil in the world and sardonic, often indecorous glosses on life and his own bitter exile in it. The third section, called, after Byron, *Hebrew Melodies (Hebräische Melodien)*, consists of three relatively long poems exploring the complex facets of Heine's revived Jewish feeling. The first, "Princess Sabbath" ("Prinzessin Sabbath") looks from without at the transformation of a poor Jew into a prince on the sabbath; the second, "Jehuda ben Halevy," is a long, rambling narrative about a poet of the great medieval Spanish Jewry, always fascinating to Heine in its dignity and elegance; and the third images a medieval disputation between a priest and rabbi before a Castilian king, whose beautiful French queen, the incarnation of the sensual, aesthetic principle, declares that both contestants "stink"—the last word of *Romanzero*.

Heine's publisher Campe was very enthusiastic about *Romanzero*. He advertised it vigorously and in his zeal invented the illustrated book jacket; *Romanzero* was the first book to have one. He published four editions virtually simultaneously and managed to sell fifteen thousand copies before the censorship bans in Austria, Prussia, and other states choked it off. The harsh, pessimistic, un-Romantic tone of *Romanzero* kept it in the shadow of the *Book of Songs* with the public at large and posterity, but many thoughtful critics have thought it the high point of Heine's poetic achievement.

However, this was not the end. There is every reason to

believe that he would have produced a fourth volume of poetry had he lived to complete it. Prostrate, with damaged eyesight, so that he could only scrawl on cardboard in pencil, in constant pain, often befogged by opiates, he continued to work on his publications in German and French, and to envision poems during his endless nights, dictating them in the daytime. In the first volume of his *Miscellaneous Writings* (*Vermischte Schriften*, 1854) he included a group of thirty-three poems, entitled *Poems 1853 and 1854 (Gedichte 1853 und 1854)*. Eleven of them are related by subtitle to the "Lazarus" cycle of *Romanzero*; among the poems he left at his death there are over a dozen more connected to the "Lazarus" theme, along with a substantial number of others, some fragmentary. The voice has become more personal and direct, but also varied: there are sardonic animal fables written for his godson, Julius Campe, Jr.; recrudescences of the old bitterness of unrequited love and assaults on Uncle Salomon and his tribe; political satires and a burlesque of Richard Wagner; powerful poems of protest, among them "The Slave Ship" ("Das Sklavenschiff"), a vision from the bleakest sources of his imagination, in which the slaves are forced to dance to retard their mortality rate on shipboard; a bitterly autobiographical fragment, "Bimini," in which he figures himself as Ponce de Leon in undignified search for the Fountain of Youth, finding only the water of death and oblivion.

And there are love poems, amazing in these circumstances. They were addressed to a rather mysterious young woman who introduced herself to him in the summer of 1855 and became a voluntary secretary. We do not know her name at birth; she was apparently the illegitimate daughter of an Austrian nobleman. Her legal name was Elise Krinitz, as she was adopted by a German family of that name, who raised her in Paris. Sometimes she called herself "Margot." In later years she published under the name of Camille Selden. Since she used an unusual seal with the image of a fly, Heine called her the "Mouche." Over a period of nine months, he wrote her twenty-five letters of love and longing, mostly urging her to come again soon. He addressed six poems to her, one of which, "Lotus Blossom" ("Lotosblume"), is included here; this and four of the others are wry love poems, full of extravagant compliment and adroitly expressed regret that the poet's physical condition prevented the consummation of their love. That was quite likely the advantage of the situation; the poetry was the safest of safe sex: "But in place of life-giving essence / All she gets to conceive is verse." He was, after all, a conspicuously married man. In 1834 he had begun to live with and in 1841 had married Crescence Eugénie Mirat, an uneducated shopgirl, whom for some reason he called "Mathilde." Heine's interpreters and biographers have not liked her very much, but he himself, though he made fun of her and complained about her alleged extravagance, expressed his love for her unremittingly until the end of his life. However, she had no access to his private realm or the wellsprings of his creativity. She knew no German and may have been no more than barely literate in French, nor had she any intellectual interests. It is not evident that she had a clear idea of what he did or of his standing in the world at large. This is, apparently, just what he wanted; he kept his inner self secluded from her as he did from his readership and his posterity. The "Mouche," on the other hand, was a partner of a different kind. She was literate in both French and German; she was poetic and sensitive, deeply read in Heine's writings; and she knew very well that she was attaching herself to an artist of world-historical significance. She was a gift to him at the rock bottom of his fortunes, a comfort in his physical pain and spiritual loneliness.

The sixth of the poems he addressed to her, thought to be the last of his life, is not a love poem but a final poetological reckoning. The poet lies in his sarcophagus while the images of Greek grace and Hebrew morality, of beauty and virtue, squabble cacophonously until their shrill uproar is drowned out by the hee-hawing of Balaam's ass. An image of prostrate marble statues being eaten away by time, "the worst syphilis," could not be printed in the nineteenth century, and nothing was known of the stanza until Camille Selden, the "Mouche," published in 1884 a French prose rendering of the poem in a memoir of Heine's last months. Thus the antinomies that energized Heine's poetry remained intact and unresolved until, in February 1856, he was released from his suffering.

The fascination of Heine's poetry has challenged translators from the middle of his career to the present day. While the French, with a prosody less compatible with that of Germanic languages, have not until quite recently attempted metrical translations but have contented themselves with prose paraphrase, there have been many attempts to make English poetry of Heine. The family relationship of the two languages is not as much of an advantage as one might suppose. Generations of translators have worried at the task of getting grammatically inflected German, with its wealth of unaccented syllables and feminine rhymes, into relatively monosyllabic English. The shorter the line and the more compact the poem, the harder it is. Heine was a poet of extreme compression; he gives the translator very little space in which to work. Furthermore, the variations of the four-line folk-song stanza, in which he wrote the majority of his poems and almost all of the most famous ones, do not have for us quite the traditional cultural dignity, the echoes of Romantic discovery, that they have in German; to us they threaten to sound like greeting-card verse. While Heine lightens and aerates an earnest tradition heavy with nationalist cultural memory, the translator into English must prove that the poetry is fundamentally serious. To these difficulties are added Heine's constant wordplay, his puns and allusions, his ingenious and sometimes outrageous rhymes.

It would not be appropriate in this place for me to impose an evaluation of the entry in this competition by Walter Arndt, a widely honored translator of profound experience. I would just venture one observation concerning his replication of Heine's rhythmic skill. Heine was a master of the counterpoint of rhythm against meter, of the flow of the spoken language against the regular alternation of iambs and trochees. In fact, this lyrical subtlety is the most reliable criterion for distinguishing a Heine poem from the rhymed prose or regimented metrical clip-clop of one of his many imitators. The effect is not easy to capture in English, and it seems to me that Walter Arndt has gone a long way toward approaching the ever receding goal with elided stresses, sprung rhythms, and hovering accents. However that may be, these efforts constitute one more contribution to what, in the eventual title of Johann Gottfried Herder's famous anthology of 1778, came to be known as *Voices of the Peoples in Song*. There cannot be too many of them.

Jeffrey L. Sammons
Spring 1995

» Selected Bibliography

DEFINITIVE EDITIONS

Historisch-kritische Gesamtausgabe der Werke, ed. Manfred Windfuhr
   et al. Hamburg: Hoffmann und Campe, 1973– .
Heinrich Heine Säkularausgabe, ed. Nationale Forschungs- und
   Gedenkstätten der klassischen deutschen Literatur in Weimar
   (renamed since German unification: Stiftung Weimarer Klassik)
   and Centre National de la Recherche Scientifique in Paris. Berlin
   and Paris: Akademie-Verlag and Editions du CNRS, 1970– .
Sämtliche Schriften, ed. Klaus Briegleb et al. Munich: Hanser,
   1968–76.

HEINE'S POETRY IN ENGLISH TRANSLATION (Selected)

Draper, Hal. *The Complete Poems of Heinrich Heine: A Modern English
   Version.* Boston: Suhrkamp/Insel, 1982.
Elliot, Alistair. *Heinrich Heine: The Lazarus Poems. With English Ver-
   sions.* Manchester: Carcanet Press, 1979.
Feise, Ernst. *Heinrich Heine: Lyric Poems and Ballads.* Pittsburgh:
   University of Pittsburgh Press, 1961.
Kramer, Aaron, et al. *The Poetry and Prose of Heinrich Heine.* Ed.
   Frederic Ewen. New York: Citadel Press, 1948.
Lazarus, Emma. *Heinrich Heine: Poems and Ballads.* New York: Wor-
   thington, 1881. Republished with illustrations by Fritz Kredel.
   New York: Hartsdale, 1947.
Untermeyer, Louis. *Heinrich Heine: Paradox and Poet.* Vol. 2: *The
   Poems.* New York: Harcourt, Brace, 1937.
Watkins, Vernon. *Heinrich Heine: The North Sea.* New York: New
   Directions, 1951.

CRITICISM IN ENGLISH (Selected)

Fairley, Barker. *Heinrich Heine: An Interpretation*. Oxford: Clarendon Press, 1954.

Hofrichter, Laura. *Heinrich Heine*. Oxford: Clarendon Press, 1963.

Perraudin, Michael. *Heinrich Heine: Poetry in Context. A Study of Buch der Lieder*. Oxford, New York, and Munich: Berg, 1989.

Peters, George F. "*Neue Gedichte*: Heine's 'Buch des Unmuts.'" In *"Der große Heide Nr. 2." Heinrich Heine and the Levels of His Goethe Reception*. New York, Bern, Frankfurt am Main, and Paris: Peter Lang, 1989.

Prawer, S. S. *Heine: Buch der Lieder*. London: Arnold, 1960.

———. *Heine the Tragic Satirist: A Study of the Later Poetry 1827–1856*. Cambridge: University Press, 1961.

Reeves, Nigel. *Heinrich Heine: Poetry and Politics*. Oxford: Oxford University Press, 1964.

Rose, William. *The Early Love Poetry of Heinrich Heine: An Inquiry into Poetic Inspiration*. Oxford: Clarendon Press, 1962.

Sammons, Jeffrey L. *Heinrich Heine: The Elusive Poet*. New Haven, Conn.: Yale University Press, 1969.

———. *Heinrich Heine: A Modern Biography*. Princeton, N.J.: Princeton University Press, 1979.

Wikoff, Jerold. *Heinrich Heine: A Study of "Neue Gedichte."* Bern: Herbert Lang; Frankfurt am Main: Peter Lang, 1975.

Youthful Sufferings

Junge Leiden

(1817–21)

》 》 》

Morgens steh ich auf und frage:
Kommt feins Liebchen heut?
Abends sink ich hin und klage:
Ausblieb sie auch heut.

In der Nacht mit meinem Kummer
Lieg' ich schlaflos, wach;
Träumend, wie im halben Schlummer,
Wandle ich bei Tag.

》 》 》

Risen in the morn, I ask:
Will she come today?
Drooping, I lament at dusk:
No—she stayed away.

In the nighttime, with my anguish
Slumberless I stay;
Only half awake, I languish
Through the dreamy day.

» Die Botschaft

Mein Knecht! steh auf und sattle schnell,
Und wirf dich auf dein Roß,
Und jage rasch durch Wald und Feld
Nach König Dunkans Schloß.

Dort schleiche in den Stall, und wart,
Bis dich der Stallbub schaut.
Den forsch mir aus: Sprich, welche ist
Von Dunkans Töchtern Braut?

Und spricht der Bub: "Die Braune ist's,"
So bring mir schnell die Mär;
Doch spricht der Bub: "Die Blonde ist's,"
So eilt das nicht so sehr.

Dann geh zum Meister Seiler hin,
Und kauf mir einen Strick,
Und reite langsam, sprich kein Wort,
Und bring mir den zurück.

» Errand

Arise, my groom, and saddle up,
On your swift courser leap
And charge apace through brush and field
Unto King Duncan's keep!

There steal into the yard and hide
About the stable quarters,
And ask the yard boy, "Which is bride
Of royal Duncan's daughters?"

If he replies "the chestnut-haired,"
Make haste to let me know;
If he replies "the golden-haired,"
You need not hasten so.

Go see the master rigger then
And buy a rope for me;
Ride home at ease, speak not a word,
And bring that back to me.

» Wasserfahrt

Ich stand gelehnet an den Mast
Und zählte jede Welle.
Ade! mein schönes Vaterland!
Mein Schiff, das segelt schnelle!

Ich kam schön Liebchens Haus vorbei,
Die Fensterscheiben blinken;
Ich guck' mir fast die Augen aus,
Doch will mir niemand winken.

Ihr Tränen, bleibt mir aus dem Aug',
Daß ich nicht dunkel sehe.
Mein krankes Herze, brich mir nicht
Vor allzugroßem Wehe.

» Taking Ship

Leaning against the mast I stood
And counted each wave that passed;
Farewell, dear native land of mine,
My ship is sailing fast!

I passed the dwelling of my love,
The windows brightly shine;
I almost gaze my eyes out, but
No waving answers mine.

You tears, do stay out of my eye,
It is too blurred to see;
My ailing heart, don't break on me,
With your burden of misery.

Lyrical Interlude

Lyrisches Intermezzo

(1822–23)

» » »

Im wunderschönen Monat Mai,
Als alle Knospen sprangen,
Da ist in meinem Herzen
Die Liebe aufgegangen.

Im wunderschönen Monat Mai,
Als alle Vögel sangen,
Da hab' ich ihr gestanden
Mein Sehnen und Verlangen.

》 》 》

In the enchanting month of May,
When all the blossoms start,
I came to feel the burgeoning
Of love within my heart.

In the enchanting month of May,
When all the songbirds choir,
I ventured to disclose to her
My longing and desire.

Die Lotosblume ängstigt
Sich vor der Sonne Pracht,
Und mit gesenktem Haupte
Erwartet sie träumend die Nacht.

Der Mond, der ist ihr Buhle,
Er weckt sie mit seinem Licht,
Und ihm entschleiert sie freundlich
Ihr frommes Blumengesicht.

Sie blüht und glüht und leuchtet
Und starret stumm in die Höh;
Sie duftet und weinet und zittert
Vor Liebe und Liebesweh.

》 》 》

The sun-god's fierce resplendence
Strikes the lotus with fright,
She drops her head of petals
And dreamily waits for the night.

The moon, he is her lover,
He rouses her with his rays,
To him she kindly uncovers
Her guileless flower face.

She blooms and glows and gazes
Mutely aloft for his sake;
Fragrant and tearful and trembling
With loving and lover's ache.

》 》 》

Du liebst mich nicht, du liebst mich nicht,
Das kümmert mich gar wenig;
Schau ich dir nur ins Angesicht,
So bin ich froh wie'n König.

Du hassest, hassest mich sogar,
So spricht dein rotes Mündchen;
Reich es mir nur zum Küssen dar,
So tröst ich mich, mein Kindchen.

》 》 》

Your dour refrain "I love you not"
But little sorrow brings;
When I but see your face, my lot
Is happy like a king's.

You hate me, loathe me, lovely miss,
Your rosy lips will scold;
Just turn them up for me to kiss
And I'll be quite consoled.

Wir haben viel für einander gefühlt,
Und dennoch uns gar vortrefflich vertragen.
Wir haben oft "Mann und Frau" gespielt,
Und dennoch uns nicht gerauft und geschlagen.
Wir haben zusammen gejauchzt und gescherzt,
Und zärtlich uns geküßt und geherzt.
Wir haben am Ende aus kindischer Lust
"Verstecken" gespielt in Wäldern und Gründen,
Und haben uns so zu verstecken gewußt,
Daß wir uns nimmermehr wiederfinden.

》 》 》

We felt a good deal for each other,
Yet got on splendidly, heaven knows;
We often played "husband and wife" together,
Yet didn't inflict either scratches or blows;
We traded banter and frolicked and mugged,
And tenderly kissed each other and hugged.
At last we agreed in a sportive mood
To play "hide and seek" in thicket and wood,
And managed to hide so cleverly then
We never can find each other again.

》 》 》

Ein Fichtenbaum steht einsam
Im Norden auf kahler Höh.
Ihn schläfert; mit weißer Decke
Umhüllen ihn Eis und Schnee.

Er träumt von einer Palme,
Die fern im Morgenland
Einsam und schweigend trauert
Auf brennender Felsenwand.

» » »

A single fir stands lonesome
On barren northernly height.
He drowses; frost and snowstorm
Shroud him in swathes of white.

He dreams about a palm—she,
In the orient far, alone,
Sorrowing stands and silent
At a blazing scarp of stone.

» » »

Aus meinen großen Schmerzen
Mach' ich die kleinen Lieder;
Die heben ihr klingend Gefieder
Und flattern nach ihrem Herzen.

Sie fanden den Weg zur Trauten,
Doch kommen sie wieder und klagen,
Und klagen, und wollen nicht sagen,
Was sie im Herzen schauten.

» » »

Out of my aching smart
I fashion my little songs;
They lift their melodious wings
And flutter their way to her heart.

They found their way to my lovely,
But they return and moan;
They moan and refuse to own
What in her heart they uncovered.

》》》

Sie haben mich gequälet,
Geärgert blau und blaß.
Die Einen mit ihrer Liebe,
Die Andern mit ihrem Haß.

Sie haben das Brot mir vergiftet,
Sie gossen mir Gift ins Glas,
Die Einen mit ihrer Liebe,
Die Andern mit ihrem Haß.

Doch sie, die mich am meisten
Gequält, geärgert, betrübt,
Die hat mich nie gehasset
Und hat mich nie geliebt.

》 》 》

They have tormented and vexed me
Into a frantic state,
The ones with their loving affection,
The others with their hate.

They dosed my drink with venom,
They poisoned the bread I ate,
The ones with their loving affection,
The others with their hate.

But she who was my vexation
And sorrow, all others above,
She never showed me hatred,
And never showed me love.

》》》

Vergiftet sind meine Lieder—
Wie könnt' es anders sein?
Du hast mir ja Gift gegossen
Ins blühende Leben hinein.

Vergiftet sind meine Lieder—
Wie könnt' es anders sein?
Ich trage im Herzen viel Schlangen,
Und dich, Geliebte mein.

》 》 》

Envenomed are my songs,
How could it be otherwise, tell?
Since you trickled poison
Into my life's clear well.

Envenomed are my songs,
How could it be otherwise, tell?
My heart holds many serpents,
And you, my love, as well.

» » »

Mir träumte wieder der alte Traum:
Es war eine Nacht im Maie,
Wir saßen unter dem Lindenbaum
Und schwuren uns ewige Treue.

Das war ein Schwören und Schwören aufs neu,
Eine Kichern, eine Kosen, ein Küssen;
Daß ich gedenk des Schwures sei,
Hast du in die Hand mich gebissen.

O Liebchen mit den Äuglein klar!
O Liebchen schön und bissig!
Das Schwören in der Ordnung war,
Das Beißen war überflüssig.

» » »

I dreamt the same old dream again:
It was on a night in May,
We sat beneath the linden then,
Pledging eternal faith.

What swearing went on between us both,
Giggles, caresses no end;
To help me be mindful of my oath,
You bit me in the hand.

O sweetheart of the gazes bright!
O fair and mordant one!
The swearing part was fine and right,
The biting was overdone.

» » »

Philister in Sonntagsröcklein
Spazieren durch Wald und Flur;
Sie jauchzen, sie hüpfen wie Böcklein,
Begrüßen die schöne Natur.

Betrachten mit blinzelnden Augen
Wie alles romantisch blüht;
Mit langen Ohren saugen
Sie ein der Spatzen Lied.

Ich aber verhänge die Fenster
Des Zimmers mit schwarzem Tuch;
Es machen mir meine Gespenster
Sogar einen Tagesbesuch.

Die alte Liebe erscheinet,
Sie stieg aus dem Totenreich;
Sie setzt sich zu mir und weinet,
Und macht das Herz mir weich.

Burghers in Sunday jerkins
Stalk wood and meadow here,
They yodel, they gambol like lambkins,
Saluting the spring of the year.

They glimpse through rheumy tears
The blossoms' romantic throng,
Through long and furry ears
They suck in the sparrows' song.

But I with sable draping
Smother my windows all;
My personal specters pay me
Even a daytime call.

My long-lost love reappears,
Ascended from realms apart,
Sits down with me in tears
And softens again my heart.

Ein Jüngling liebt ein Mädchen,
Die hat einen andern erwählt;
Der andre liebt eine andre
Und hat sich mit dieser vermählt.

Das Mädchen heiratet aus Ärger
Den ersten besten Mann,
Der ihr in den Weg gelaufen;
Der Jüngling ist übel dran.

Es ist eine alte Geschichte,
Doch bleibt sie immer neu;
Und wem sie just passieret,
Dem bricht das Herz entzwei.

A young man loves a maiden,
Who chose another instead;
That other loves another
And led her to altar and bed.

The maiden in her anger
Weds the first likely lad
That happened to come across her;
The young man's lot is sad.

It is a time-worn story,
And yet it is ever new;
And when it happens to someone
It breaks his heart in two.

» » »

Am leuchtenden Sommermorgen
Geh ich im Garten herum.
Es flüstern und sprechen die Blumen,
Ich aber, ich wandle stumm.

Es flüstern und sprechen die Blumen,
Und schaun mitleidig mich an:
Sei unserer Schwester nicht böse,
Du trauriger, blasser Mann!

》 》 》

This radiant morning of summer
I walk in the flowering yard;
The blossoms whisper and gossip,
I walk with never a word.

The blossoms gossip and whisper
And watch me regretful and sad:
"Do not be cross with our sister,
You pallid, sorrowing lad!"

Allnächtlich im Traume seh ich dich,
Und sehe dich freundlich grüßen,
Und lautaufweinend stürz ich mich
Zu deinen süßen Füßen.

Du siehst mich an wehmütiglich,
Und schüttelst das blonde Köpfchen;
Aus deinen Augen schleichen sich
Die Perlentränentröpfchen.

Du sagst mir heimlich ein leises Wort,
Und gibst mir den Strauß von Zypressen.
Ich wache auf, und der Strauß ist fort,
Und das Wort hab ich vergessen.

》》》

I see you in my dream each night
And watch you graciously greet;
I sob out loud upon the sight
And throw myself at your feet.

You gaze so ruefully at me
And shake your fair head of curls,
And from your eyelids furtively
The teardrops seep like pearls.

You give me a secret word anon
And your posy from cypress twined.
When I wake up, the posy is gone,
And the word has slipped my mind.

Der Herbstwind rüttelt die Bäume,
Die Nacht ist feucht und kalt;
Gehüllt im grauen Mantel,
Reite ich einsam im Wald.

Und wie ich reite, so reiten
Mir die Gedanken voraus;
Die tragen mich leicht und luftig
Nach meiner Liebsten Haus.

Die Hunde bellen, die Diener
Erscheinen mit Kerzengeflirr;
Die Wendeltreppe stürm ich
Hinauf mir Sporengeklirr.

Im leuchtenden Teppichgemache,
Da ist es so duftig und warm,
Da harret meiner die Holde—
Ich fliege in ihren Arm.

Es säuselt der Wind in den Blättern,
Es spricht der Eichenbaum:
Was willst du, törichter Reiter,
Mit deinem törichten Traum?

The night is damp and chilly,
The fall wind rattles the trees;
I ride alone in the forest,
Wrapped in my gray pelisse.

And as I ride, my musings
Travel ahead above;
They carry me, light and airy,
To the house of my lady-love.

The dogs give voice, the servants
Step out, lights shimmering.
I storm up the spiral staircase,
My rowels jingle and ring.

In the lustrous carpeted chamber
It is so fragrant and warm;
And there my love awaits me—
I fly into her arms.

Now murmurs the wind in the leafage,
And the creaking oak limbs seem
To ask: "Mad horseman, what would you
With that nonsensical dream?"

Homecoming

Die Heimkehr

(1823–24)

» Die Lorelei

Ich weiß nicht, was soll es bedeuten,
Daß ich so traurig bin;
Ein Märchen aus alten Zeiten,
Das kommt mir nicht aus dem Sinn.

Die Luft ist kühl und es dunkelt,
Und ruhig fließt der Rhein;
Der Gipfel des Berges funkelt
Im Abendsonnenschein.

Die schönste Jungfrau sitzet
Dort oben wunderbar,
Ihr goldnes Geschmeide blitzet,
Sie kämmt ihr goldenes Haar.

Sie kämmt es mit goldenem Kamme
Und singt ein Lied dabei,
Das hat eine wundersame,
Gewaltige Melodei.

Den Schiffer im kleinen Schiffe
Ergreift es mit wildem Weh;
Er schaut nicht die Felsenriffe,
Er schaut nur hinauf in die Höh'.

Ich glaube, die Wellen verschlingen
Am Ende Schiffer und Kahn;
Und das hat mit ihrem Singen
Die Lorelei getan.

» Lorelei

I wonder what it presages—
I am so sad at heart;
A legend of bygone ages
Haunts me and will not depart.

The air is cool, and it darkles,
And calmly courses the Rhine.
The peak of the mountain sparkles
As evening rays on it shine.

The fairest maid is seated
All wrapt in enchantment there;
Gems gleam on her, gold-ensheeted,
She combs her golden hair.

She combs with a comb that is golden
And sings a song withal,
Its strain is of spell-enfolding,
All-overpowering thrall.

The skipper in his poor schooner
Is seized with a savage woe;
Would gaze at the summit sooner
Than down at the reefs below.

I think the waves must devour
Both skipper and ship ere long;
Which came to pass by the power
Of Lorelei and her song.

Mein Herz, mein Herz ist traurig,
Doch lustig leuchtet der Mai;
Ich stehe, gelehnt an der Linde,
Hoch auf der alten Bastei.

Da drunten fließt der blaue
Stadtgraben in stiller Ruh';
Ein Knabe fährt im Kahne,
Und angelt und pfeift dazu.

Jenseits erheben sich freundlich,
In winziger, bunter Gestalt,
Lusthäuser, und Gärten, und Menschen,
Und Ochsen, und Wiesen, und Wald.

Die Mägde bleichen Wäsche,
Und springen im Gras herum;
Das Mühlrad stäubt Diamanten,
Ich höre sein fernes Gesumm'.

Am alten grauen Turme
Ein Schilderhäuschen steht;
Ein rotgeröckter Bursche
Dort auf und nieder geht.

Er spielt mit seiner Flinte,
Die funkelt im Sonnenrot,
Er präsentiert und schultert—
Ich wollt, er schösse mich tot.

》》》

My heart, my heart is heavy,
Yet May so gaily blooms;
I lean against the linden
Where the old bastion looms.

Far down, the quiet town moat
Trails blue waters along;
On it a boy in a rowboat
Is fishing and whistling a song.

Yonder, a charming vista
In colorful miniature mood:
Gardens, pavilions, and people,
And oxen and meadows and wood.

The maids are bleaching linen
And skipping about on the green;
The millwheel sends diamonds skimming,
I hear its hum where I lean.

Up by the old gray tower
They have a sentry booth;
A lad in a scarlet tunic
Is pacing back and forth.

He is toying with his weapon,
It gleams in the sunshine's red;
Presenting and should'ring the rifle—
I wish he would shoot me dead.

Wir saßen am Fischerhause,
Und schauten nach der See;
Die Abendnebel kamen,
Und stiegen in die Höh'.

Im Leuchtturm wurden die Lichter
Allmählig angesteckt,
Und in der weiten Ferne
Ward noch ein Schiff entdeckt.

Wir sprachen von Sturm und Schiffbruch,
Vom Seemann, und wie er lebt,
Und zwischen Himmel und Wasser
Und Angst und Freude schwebt.

Wir sprachen von fernen Küsten,
Vom Süden und vom Nord,
Und von den seltsamen Völkern
Und seltsamen Sitten dort.

Am Ganges duftet's und leuchtet's,
Und Riesenbäume blühn,
Und schöne, stille Menschen
Vor Lotosblumen knien.

In Lappland sind schmutzige Leute,
Plattköpfig, breitmäulig und klein;
Sie kauern ums Feuer, und backen
Sich Fische, und quäken und schrein.

We sat by the fisherman's cottage
And gazed where the tideline spread.
The evening mists were brewing
And rising overhead.

The lanterns of the lighthouse
Were one by one turned on,
And dimly in the distance,
Belated, a sailship shone.

We spoke of storm and shipwreck,
Of sailor's life and employ,
And how 'twixt sky and water
He hovers, and fear and joy.

We spoke of far-off shorelines,
Of southern and northern bays,
And of the peculiar folk there
And their peculiar ways.

The Ganges, all blaze and fragrance,
Where blossoming trees loom up,
And beautiful quiet people
Kneel to the lotus cup.

In Lappland people are dirty,
Flat-headed, wide-muzzled, small,
They squat by the campfire, baking
Their catch, and they bray and squall.

Die Mädchen horchten ernsthaft,
Und endlich sprach niemand mehr;
Das Schiff war nicht mehr sichtbar,
Es dunkelte gar zu sehr.

The maidens listened gravely,
And nobody spoke at last;
The vessel was seen no longer,
The light was failing too fast.

Du schönes Fischermädchen,
Treibe den Kahn ans Land,
Komm zu mir und setze dich nieder,
Wir kosen Hand in Hand.

Leg an mein Herz dein Köpfchen,
Und fürchte dich nicht so sehr;
Vertraust du dich doch furchtlos
Täglich dem wilden Meer.

Mein Herz gleicht ganz dem Meere,
Hat Sturm und Ebb' und Flut,
Und manche schöne Perle
In seiner Tiefe ruht.

You lovely fisher-maiden
Paddle your boat to land,
Come here, sit down beside me,
We'll dally hand in hand.

Against my heart more bravely
Nestle your head; dear me,
Think how unfearing, daily,
You trust in the savage sea.

My heart is just like the ocean,
Has storm and calm and tides,
And many a pearl of beauty
Upon its bed resides.

» » »

Wenn ich an deinem Hause
Des Morgens vorüber geh',
So freut's mich, du liebe Kleine,
Wenn ich dich am Fenster seh'.

Mit deinen schwarzbraunen Augen
Siehst du mich forschend an:
Wer bist du, und was fehlt dir,
Du fremder, kranker Mann?

"Ich bin ein deutscher Dichter,
Bekannt im deutschen Land;
Nennt man die besten Namen,
So wird auch der meine genannt.

Und was mir fehlt, du Kleine,
Fehlt manchem im deutschen Land;
Nennt man die schlimmsten Schmerzen,
So wird auch der meine genannt."

》》》

When of a morning early
I happen to pass your place,
I am happy to see you, dear girlie,
Stand at the window case.

Your gazes from dark-brown eyes
Earnestly probe me and scan:
Who are you and what ails you,
You strange and suffering man?

"I am a German poet
Well-known in the German world;
Where the foremost names are mentioned,
My name is also heard.

"And what ails me, little dearie,
Ails many in Germany;
Among the most sorely stricken
They also mention me."

Das Meer erglänzte weit hinaus
Im letzten Abendscheine;
Wir saßen am einsamen Fischerhaus,
Wir saßen stumm und alleine.

Der Nebel stieg, das Wasser schwoll,
Die Möwe flog hin und wieder;
Aus deinen Augen, liebevoll,
Fielen die Tränen nieder.

Ich sah sie fallen auf deine Hand,
Und bin aufs Knie gesunken;
Ich hab von deiner weißen Hand
Die Tränen fortgetrunken.

Seit jener Stunde verzehrt sich mein Leib,
Die Seele stirbt vor Sehnen;—
Mich hat das unglückselge Weib
Vergiftet mit ihren Tränen.

The sea was aglitter far and wide
As the last of the sunset shone:
We sat by the lonely cabin's side
Sat silent and alone.

The seagull rode the sky above,
Higher rose mist and swell;
While in your eyes, so full of love,
The teardrops brimmed and fell.

I saw them fall upon your hand
And dropped upon one knee;
And bending over your pallid hand,
I sipped your tears away.

Since then, my flesh has shrunk, sad lust
Tortures my soul and sears;
Alas, the wretched woman must
Have poisoned me with her tears.

Am fernen Horizonte
Erscheint, wie ein Nebelbild,
Die Stadt mit ihren Türmen
In Abenddämmrung gehüllt.

Ein feuchter Windzug kräuselt
Die graue Wasserbahn;
Mit traurigem Takte rudert
Der Schiffer in meinem Kahn.

Die Sonne hebt sich noch einmal
Leuchtend vom Boden empor,
Und zeigt mir jene Stelle,
Wo ich das Liebste verlor.

》》》

As part of the distant horizon
There looms like a vapor-scape
The city with towers and spires,
A twilight-shrouded shape.

A moisty sea breeze ruffles
The grayish water space;
The oarsman in my wherry
Strokes at a cheerless pace.

For one last time the sun disk
Will glowingly reappear,
Marking to me the setting
Where I lost what I held most dear.

》 》 》

Ich stand in dunklen Träumen
Und starrte ihr Bildnis an,
Und das geliebte Antlitz
Heimlich zu leben begann.

Um ihre Lippen zog sich
Ein Lächeln wunderbar,
Und wie von Wehmutstränen
Erglänzte ihr Augenpaar.

Auch meine Tränen flossen
Mir von den Wangen herab—
Und ach, ich kann es nicht glauben,
Daß ich dich verloren hab!

I stood in somber musing,
Willing her portrait alive,
When her beloved likeness
Secretly seemed to revive.

About her lips there grew
A smile in wondrous wise,
And as with tears of rue
Shimmered her lovely eyes.

By then I felt from my own eyes
The tears of sorrow spill—
That I should have lost you—Heaven!
I cannot believe it still!

» » »

Sie liebten sich beide, doch keiner
Wollt es dem andern gestehn;
Sie sahen sich an so feindlich,
Und wollten vor Liebe vergehn.

Sie trennten sich endlich und sahn sich
Nur noch zuweilen im Traum;
Sie waren längst gestorben,
Und wußten es selber kaum.

» » »

They bore a love for each other
Which neither had spoken of;
Each had cold looks for the other
While being consumed with love.

They parted at last and since then
Only in dreams still met;
They had died the Lord knows when,
But were not aware of it yet.

» » »

Und als ich euch meine Schmerzen geklagt,
Da habt ihr gegähnt und nichts gesagt;
Doch als ich sie zierlich in Verse gebracht,
Da habt ihr mir große Elogen gemacht.

》》》

The time I came to you with my plaints,
You gave me yawns and nothing more;
But when I cast them in graceful quatrains,
You paid me compliments galore.

» » »

Mensch, verspotte nicht den Teufel,
Kurz ist ja die Lebensbahn,
Und die ewige Verdammnis
Ist kein bloßer Pöbelwahn.

Mensch, bezahle deine Schulden,
Lang ist ja die Lebensbahn,
Und du mußt noch manchmal borgen,
Wie du es so oft getan.

》》》

Man, do not deride the Devil,
For your run on earth is brief,
And perpetual damnation
Is no vulgar folk belief.

Man, pay back the debts you owe,
You still face a lengthy run,
And you'll have again to borrow,
As you have so often done.

» » »

Mein Kind, wir waren Kinder,
Zwei Kinder, klein und froh;
Wir krochen ins Hühnerhäuschen,
Versteckten uns unter das Stroh.

Wir krähten wie die Hähne,
Und kamen Leute vorbei—
Kikereküh! Sie glaubten,
Es wäre Hahnengeschrei.

Die Kisten auf unserem Hofe,
Die tapezierten wir aus,
Und wohnten drin beisammen,
Und machten ein vornehmes Haus.

Des Nachbars alte Katze
Kam öfters zum Besuch;
Wir machten ihr Bückling' und Knickse
Und Komplimente genug.

Wir haben nach ihrem Befinden
Besorglich und freundlich gefragt;
Wir haben seitdem dasselbe
Mancher alten Katze gesagt.

Wir saßen auch oft und sprachen
Vernünftig, wie alte Leut',
Und klagten, wie alles besser
Gewesen zu unserer Zeit.

We two, my dear, were children,
Two children merry and small,
We crawled into the henhouse
And hid beneath the straw.

We crowed just like two roosters—
When people happened by,
"Cocklededoo!" They took it
For a real live rooster cry.

The boxes in our backyard
We lined with papier-mâché
And went to live there, keeping
A household most distingué.

The neighbor's old cat came calling
And asked to be let in the door;
We bowed and scraped in her honor
With compliments galore.

We earnestly inquired
Of her spirits and health and all that;
We have said the same things later
To many another old cat.

Often we sat there, talking
In sensible old folks' tongue,
Complaining how all was better
Back then when we were young.

Wie Lieb' und Treu' und Glauben
Verschwunden aus der Welt,
Und wie so teuer der Kaffee,
Und wie so rar das Geld!

Vorbei sind die Kinderspiele,
Und alles rollt vorbei—
Das Geld und die Welt und die Zeiten,
Und Glauben und Lieb' und Treu'.

How love and faith and honor
Had disappeared from the earth,
How the price of coffee had risen,
And how little a mark was worth.

Gone are the childish pretendings,
And everything else rolls past,
Money and world and eras,
And faith and love and trust.

» » »

Im Traum sah ich die Geliebte,
Ein banges, bekümmertes Weib,
Verwelkt und abgefallen
Der sonst so blühende Leib.

Ein Kind trug sie auf dem Arme,
Ein andres führt sie an der Hand,
Und sichtbar ist Armut und Trübsal
Am Gang und Blick und Gewand.

Sie schwankte über den Marktplatz,
Und da begegnet sie mir,
Und sieht mich an, und ruhig
Und schmerzlich sag ich zu ihr:

Komm mit nach meinem Hause,
Denn du bist blaß und krank;
Ich will durch Fleiß und Arbeit
Dir schaffen Speis' und Trank.

Ich will auch pflegen und warten
Die Kinder, die bei dir sind,
Vor allem aber dich selber,
Du armes, unglückliches Kind.

Ich will dir nie erzählen,
Daß ich dich geliebet hab,
Und wenn du stirbst, so will ich
Weinen auf deinem Grab.

In a dream I saw the beloved,
A woman worn and downcast,
Haggard and raddled the body
So blooming and fresh in the past.

A baby clasped to her shoulder,
A boy by the hand held she;
Posture and gaze and attire
Spoke sorrow and penury.

She totters across the marketplace
And now encounters me there;
She looks at me, and calmly
And sadly I say to her:

"Come to my house with me,
By striving and toil I will
Provide you with food and drink—
For you are pale and ill.

"I'll also look after and care for
These children and keep them safe;
Above all else yourself, though,
You poor unhappy waif.

"And I will never tell you
Of your love that once I found,
And when you die, I will be
Weeping upon your mound."

» » »

Herz, mein Herz, sei nicht beklommen,
Und ertrage dein Geschick.
Neuer Frühling gibt zurück,
Was der Winter dir genommen.

Und wie viel ist dir geblieben!
Und wie schön ist noch die Welt!
Und, mein Herz, was dir gefällt,
Alles, alles darfst du lieben!

》》》

Heart, my heart, be not discouraged
And accept what is your fate;
Spring's return will re-create
What the wintertime has ravished.

Think what world is left you still,
And how lovely is that part;
All, yes, all you like, my heart,
Is for you to love at will!

Du bist wie eine Blume,
So hold und schön und rein;
Ich schau dich an, und Wehmut
Schleicht mir ins Herz hinein.

Mir ist, als ob ich die Hände
Aufs Haupt dir legen sollt,
Betend, daß Gott dich erhalte
So rein und schön und hold.

》 》 》

You blossom like a flower,
So fair and pure and whole;
I gaze at you, and sadness
Steals into my soul.

I feel I should be laying
My hands upon your hair,
Praying that God may preserve you
So whole and pure and fair.

Kind! Es wäre dein Verderben,
Und ich geb mir selber Mühe,
Daß dein liebes Herz in Liebe
Nimmermehr für mich erglühe.

Nur daß mir's so leicht gelinget,
Will mich dennoch fast betrüben,
Und ich denke manchmal dennoch:
Möchtest du mich dennoch lieben!

» » »

Child: it would be your undoing;
I myself take pains to see
That your little heart should never
Catch on fire with love for me.

Yet the fact it comes so easy
Does not sit with me at all;
And I catch myself half hoping
You will love me after all.

» » »

Ich wollte bei dir weilen
Und an deiner Seite ruhn;
Du mußtest von mir eilen;
Du hattest viel zu tun.

Ich sagte, daß meine Seele
Dir gänzlich ergeben sei;
Du lachtest aus voller Kehle,
Und machtest 'nen Knicks dabei.

Du hast noch mehr gesteigert
Mir meinen Liebesverdruß,
Und hast mir sogar verweigert
Am Ende den Abschiedskuß.

Glaub nicht, daß ich mich erschieße,
Wie schlimm auch die Sachen stehn!
Das alles, meine Süße,
Ist mir schon einmal geschehn.

» » »

I had in mind to stay
And rest for a while with you;
You had to hurry away;
You had a lot to do.

I said my soul was devoutly
And wholly under your spell;
Your burst out laughing loudly
And bobbed me a curtsey as well.

And ever more you defied me
To find even bitter bliss;
And finally you denied me
Even the farewell kiss.

Don't think I will shoot myself,
My heart be ever so sore!
All this, you know, sweet elf,
Has happened to me before.

Saphire sind die Augen dein,
Die lieblichen, die süßen.
Oh, dreimal glücklich ist der Mann,
Den sie mit Liebe grüßen.

Dein Herz, es ist ein Diamant,
Der edle Lichter sprühet.
Oh, dreimal glücklich ist der Mann,
Für den es liebend glühet.

Rubinen sind die Lippen dein,
Man kann nicht schönre sehen.
Oh, dreimal glücklich ist der Mann,
Dem sie die Liebe gestehen.

Oh, kennt ich nur den glücklichen Mann,
Oh, daß ich ihn nur fände,
So recht allein im grünen Wald,
Sein Glück hätt' bald ein Ende.

》 》 》

Sapphires are those eyes of yours,
Ravishingly sweet,
Oh, triply fortunate the man
Whom lovingly they greet.

Your heart is like the diamond
That sparkles noble beams;
Oh, triply lucky is the man
For whom with love it gleams.

Your lips are like twin ruby stones,
None lovelier anywhere;
Oh, triply fortunate the man
To whom they love aver.

Oh, if I knew this lucky man
And found him thus in clover,
Just tête-à-tête in the deep green wood,
His luck would soon be over.

》》》

Zu fragmentarisch ist Welt und Leben!
Ich will mich zum deutschen Professor begeben.
Der weiß das Leben zusammenzusetzen,
Und er macht ein verständlich System daraus;
Mit seinen Nachtmützen und Schlafrockfetzen
Stopft er die Lücken des Weltenbaus.

World and life are disjoint and awry!
To the German professor let me apply.
He can assemble life, bit by bit,
And make a rational system of it.
With his nightcaps and shreds of his raggedy robe
He plugs the gaps in the heavenly globe.

Ich wollt, meine Schmerzen ergössen
Sich all in ein einziges Wort,
Das gäb ich den lustigen Winden,
Die trügen es lustig fort.

Sie tragen zu dir, Geliebte,
Das schmerzerfüllte Wort;
Du hörst es zu jeder Stunde,
Du hörst es an jedem Ort.

Und hast du zum nächtlichen Schlummer
Geschlossen die Augen kaum,
So wird dich mein Wort verfolgen
Bis in den tiefsten Traum.

》 》 》

I wish my heart's chagrins
Were poured in a single word,
I'd launch it on the gay winds,
They'd carry it merrily forth.

To you they carry, beloved,
That pain-charged word from afar;
You hear it hour upon hour,
You hear it wherever you are.

And barely you may have lowered
Your eyelids to slumber—in vain;
Deep in your dreams you will be
Pursued by that word of pain.

Du hast Diamanten und Perlen,
Hast alles, was Menschenbegehr,
Und hast die schönsten Augen—
Mein Liebchen, was willst du mehr?

Auf deine schönen Augen
Hab ich ein ganzes Heer
Von ewigen Liedern gedichtet—
Mein Liebchen, was willst du mehr?

Mit deinen schönen Augen
Hast du mich gequält so sehr,
Und hast mich zu Grunde gerichtet—
Mein Liebchen, was willst du mehr?

》 》 》

You have diamonds, you have pearls,
You have all that heart may crave;
You have the most beautiful eyes;
My lovely, what more would you have?

In praise of your beautiful eyes
I have launched an entire fleet
Of deathless poems—my dear,
My lovely, what more do you need?

Those beautiful eyes of yours
Have made me suffer and bleed;
You have ruined my life, so now,
My love, what more do you need?

» » »

Gaben mir Rat und gute Lehren,
Überschütteten mich mit Ehren,
Sagten, daß ich nur warten sollt,
Haben mich protegieren gewollt.

Aber bei all ihrem Protegieren
Hätte ich können vor Hunger krepieren,
Wär nicht gekommen ein braver Mann,
Wacker nahm er sich meiner an.

Braver Mann! Er schafft mir zu essen!
Will es ihm nie und nimmer vergessen!
Schade, daß ich ihn nicht küssen kann!
Denn ich bin selbst dieser brave Mann.

》 》 》

They gave me counsel and words to the wise
And eulogies more than enough,
Told me to just be patient a while,
They'd intercede in my behalf.

But for all their patronages
I could have perished under bridges
Had there not come a man of heart
To look after me and take my part.

Oh worthy man! He keeps me in food!
I'll never forget his solicitude!
Ah, what shame I can't embrace him!
It's in my looking glass I face him.

» » »

Wir fuhren allein im dunkeln
Postwagen die ganze Nacht;
Wir ruhten einander am Herzen,
Wir haben gescherzt und gelacht.

Doch als es morgens tagte,
Mein Kind, wie staunten wir!
Denn zwischen uns saß Amor,
Der blinde Passagier.

》 》 》

We rode in the darkened stagecoach
All night for many a mile,
We rested our hearts on each other,
Laughing and joking the while.

But when the daylight woke us
We knew not what to say:
Between us two sat Cupid,
The furtive stowaway.

» » »

Und bist du erst mein ehlich Weib,
Dann bist du zu beneiden,
Dann lebst du in lauter Zeitvertreib,
In lauter Pläsir und Freuden.

Und wenn du schiltst und wenn du tobst,
Ich werd' es geduldig leiden;
Doch wenn du meine Verse nicht lobst,
Laß ich mich von dir scheiden.

》》》

When you're my wedded wife, you'll be
Assured a life of pleasure,
Will spend your days most enviably
In luxury and leisure.

And when you scold and when you curse,
I'll bear it and endorse you;
But if you fail to praise my verse,
By God, I shall divorce you.

》 》 》

Der Tod das ist die kühle Nacht,
Das Leben ist der schwüle Tag.
Es dunkelt schon, mich schläfert,
Der Tag hat mich müd' gemacht.

Über mein Bett erhebt sich ein Baum,
Drin singt die junge Nachtigall;
Sie singt von lauter Liebe,
Ich hör es sogar im Traum.

» » »

Death is the cool of night,
Life is the sultry day;
It's darkening, I am sleepy;
The day has tired me.

Over my bedstead rises a tree;
In it the young nightingale sings;
It sings of nothing but love—
Deep in my dreams it rings.

» » »

Zu der Lauheit und der Flauheit
Deiner Seele paßte nicht
Meiner Liebe wilde Rauheit,
Die sich Bahn durch Felsen bricht.

Du, du liebtest die Chausseen
In der Liebe, und ich schau'
Dich am Arm des Gatten gehen,
Eine brave, schwangre Frau.

》 》 》

My desire's volcanic rapid,
Blasting paths through rock and rough,
Was ill-suited to the vapid,
Tepid temper of your love.

You preferred the neatly tonsured
Parks of love; I see you now
Stroll, supported by your consort—
Dutiful and pregnant *Frau*.

New Poems

Neue Gedichte

»   Leise zieht durch mein Gemüt
Liebliches Geläute.
Klinge, kleines Frühlingslied,
Kling hinaus ins Weite.

Kling hinaus bis an das Haus,
Wo die Blumen sprießen.
Wenn du eine Rose schaust,
Sag, ich laß sie grüßen.

»   Softly through my spirit sound
        Carillons of May;
        Little song of spring, resound,
        Ring afar, away.

        Ring to reach a house I know,
        Set in flowering yards;
        When you see a rosebud blow,
        Give it my regards.

» Wenn du mir vorüberwandelst,
Und dein Kleid berührt mich nur,
Jubelt dir mein Herz, und stürmisch
Folgt es deiner schönen Spur.

Dann drehst du dich um, und schaust mich
Mit den großen Augen an,
Und mein Herz ist so erschrocken,
Daß es kaum dir folgen kann.

» When by chance you pass my station
And but brush me with your veil,
All my heart in jubilation
Bounds along your lovely trail.

Then you turn and open wide
Those two earnest eyes at me,
And my heart, now terrified,
Hardly dares to follow you.

» Mit deinen blauen Augen
Siehst du mich lieblich an,
Da wird mir so träumend zu Sinne,
Daß ich nicht sprechen kann.

An deine blauen Augen
Gedenk ich allerwärts;
Ein Meer von blauen Gedanken
Ergießt sich über mein Herz.

» From those blue eyes of yours
You send me a lovely ray;
This sets me so deeply dreaming
It takes my speech away.

Those blue-blue eyes of yours
Pursue me and will not depart;
A sea of blue thoughts surging
And breaking over my heart.

》   Ich wandle unter Blumen
Und blühe selber mit;
Ich wandle wie im Traume
Und schwanke bei jedem Schritt.

Oh, halt mich fest, Geliebte!
Vor Liebestrunkenheit
Fall ich dir sonst zu Füßen,
Und der Garten ist voller Leut'.

» I walk in a flower garden
And seem to be blossoming too;
I wander as if dreaming
And falter each step I do.

Oh hold me fast, beloved,
Or in waves of love half-drowned,
I might fall down at your feet—
And people are all around.

» Es haben unsre Herzen
Geschlossen die heil'ge Allianz;
Sie lagen fest aneinander
Und sie verstanden sich ganz.

Ach, nur die junge Rose,
Die deine Brust geschmückt,
Die arme Bundesgenossin,
Sie wurde fast zerdrückt.

» Our hearts have concluded a pact
Of mutual trust and reliance;
They firmly clasped each other
As one, like the Holy Alliance.

But oh, the rose at your bosom
With its fresh and fragrant breath,
That luckless ally between us
Was all but squeezed to death.

»   Küsse, die man stiehlt im Dunkeln
Und im Dunkeln wiedergibt,
Solche Küsse, wie beselgen
Sie die Seele, wenn sie liebt!

Ahnend und erinnrungsüchtig
Denkt die Seele sich dabei
Manches von vergangnen Tagen,
Und von Zukunft mancherlei.

Doch das gar zu viele Denken
Ist bedenklich, wenn man küßt;—
Weine lieber, liebe Seele,
Weil das Weinen leichter ist.

» Kisses stolen in the dark,
In the dark reciprocated,
How they fill with happiness
Kindred souls by love elated!

Both recalling and divining,
Souls will be at pains to see
Many sights of days departed,
Much of what is yet to be.

In your kisses, though, be wary
Of much thinking, be on guard—
Rather weep, beloved soul,
For to weep is not as hard.

» Morgens send ich dir die Veilchen,
Die ich früh im Wald gefunden,
Und des Abends bring ich Rosen,
Die ich brach in Dämmrungsstunden.

Weißt du was die hübschen Blumen
Dir Verblümtes sagen möchten?
Treu sein sollst du mir am Tage
Und mich lieben in den Nächten.

» Morningtime, I send you violets—
Early found in dewy heather,
Evenings I bring you roses
Picked as shades of twilight gather.

Know you what the pretty flowers
Tell you in a floral key?
Be you faithful in the daytime,
Loving in the night with me.

» 　　Der Brief, den du geschrieben,
Er macht mich gar nicht bang;
Du willst mich nicht mehr lieben,
Aber dein Brief ist lang.

Zwölf Seiten, eng und zierlich!
Ein kleines Manuskript!
Man schreibt nicht so ausführlich,
Wenn man den Abschied gibt.

» The letter that you wrote me
Occasions me no grief;
You're out of love, you wrote me,
But you were hardly brief.

Twelve pages, crammed unduly
With calligraphic stuff!
One doesn't write so fully
When one is breaking off.

» Die holden Wünsche blühen,
Und welken wieder ab,
Und blühen und welken wieder—
So geht es bis ans Grab.

Das weiß ich, und das vertrübet
Mir alle Lieb' und Lust;
Mein Herz ist so klug und witzig,
Und verblutet in meiner Brust.

》   The lovely wishes blossom
     And then they wilt again;
     By turns they blossom and wither,
     And so down boneyard lane.

     I know this, and it overshadows
     All of my love and zest;
     My heart is so clever and witty,
     And bleeds to death in my breast.

» Himmel grau und wochentäglich!
Auch die Stadt ist noch dieselbe!
Und noch immer blöd und kläglich
Spiegelt sie sich in der Elbe.

Lange Nasen, noch langweilig
Werden sie wie sonst geschneuzet,
Und das duckt sich noch scheinheilig,
Oder bläht sich, stolz gespreizet.

Schöner Süden! wie verehr ich
Deinen Himmel, deine Götter,
Seit ich diesen Menschenkehricht
Wiederseh, und dieses Wetter!

» Heavens gray and workday-dismal!
City, too, the same as ever!
Still as witless and abysmal
Mirrored in the Elbe River.

Noses long, with dreary rumble
Into handkerchiefs discharging,
Humans crouching, falsely humble,
Or presumptuously barging.

Lovely South! Oh, how I worship
Your mild gods, your heavens blue,
Having faced this human garbage
And its hopeless clime anew!

» Anno 1829

Daß ich bequem verbluten kann,
Gebt mir ein edles, weites Feld!
O, laßt mich nicht ersticken hier
In dieser engen Krämerwelt!

Sie essen gut, sie trinken gut,
Erfreun sich ihres Maulwurfglücks,
Und ihre Großmut ist so groß
Als wie das Loch der Armenbüchs.

Zigarren tragen sie im Maul
Und in der Hosentasch' die Händ';
Auch die Verdauungskraft ist gut—
Wer sie nur selbst verdauen könnt!

Sie handeln mit den Spezerei'n
Der ganzen Welt, doch in der Luft,
Trotz allen Würzen, riecht man stets
Den faulen Schellfischseelenduft.

O, daß ich große Laster säh,
Verbrechen, blutig, kolossal—
Nur diese satte Tugend nicht,
Und zahlungsfähige Moral!

» Anno 1829

Grant me a noble, spacious plain,
To bleed to death in comfort there!
Let me not fight for breath in vain
In this provincial peddler's lair!

They gobble well, they guzzle well,
They bless their marmot's lot;
Their generosity is broad
Just like a poor-box slot.

Cigars are planted in their snouts,
Hands in their pocket-wells;
Their stomachs prosper—but who can
Stomach these gents themselves?

They trade in spice and condiments
From East and West, and yet there winds,
Through all the fragrances one scents,
The rotten-fish smell of their minds.

Oh were there grandiose transgressions,
Prodigious, blood-stained villainy,
In place of this complacent virtue,
This smugly moral solvency!

Ihr Wolken droben, nehmt mich mit,
Gleichviel nach welchem fernen Ort!
Nach Lappland oder Afrika,
Und sei's nach Pommern—fort! nur fort!

O, nehmt mich mit—Sie hören nicht—
Die Wolken droben sind so klug!
Vorüberreisend dieser Stadt,
Ängstlich beschleun'gen sie den Flug.

Oh clouds aloft, take me afar,
Whatever distant course you fare!
To Lappland or to Africa,
Why, Pomerania! I don't care!

Oh take me off! They do not hear.
Those clouds above me are too shrewd:
As they come floating by this town,
They flinch, and raise their altitude.

» Anno 1839

O Deutschland, meine ferne Liebe,
Gedenk ich deiner, wein ich fast!
Das muntre Frankreich scheint mir trübe,
Das leichte Volk wird mir zur Last.

Nur der Verstand, so kalt und trocken,
Herrscht in dem witzigen Paris—
O, Narrheitsglöcklein, Glaubensglocken,
Wie klingelt ihr daheim so süß!

Höfliche Männer! Doch verdrossen
Geb ich den art'gen Gruß zurück.—
Die Grobheit, die ich einst genossen
Im Vaterland, das war mein Glück!

Lächelnde Weiber! Plappern immer,
Wie Mühlenräder stets bewegt!
Do lob ich Deutschlands Frauenzimmer,
Das schweigend sich zu Bette legt.

Und alles dreht sich hier im Kreise,
Mit Ungestüm, wie 'n toller Traum!
Bei uns bleibt alles hübsch im Gleise,
Wie angenagelt, rührt sich kaum.

Mir ist, als hört' ich fern erklingen
Nachtwächterhörner, sanft und traut;
Nachtwächterlieder hör ich singen,
Dazwischen Nachtigallenlaut.

Oh Germany, my far-off dear,
I all but weep to think of thee!
Light-hearted France seems drab and drear,
Her giddy race depresses me.

Mere logic, frigidly sublime,
Rules clever Paris all alone;
Oh foolscap jingles, church-bells' chime,
How sweetly you resound at home!

Such civil gentlemen! But sourly
Do I return their suave address—
The churlishness encountered hourly
In Germany was happiness!

These smiling women! Always prating,
Like waterwheels forever stirred!
How I prefer the German maiden,
Who comes to bed without a word.

Here everything is whirling, flailing,
Flung headlong in a crazy round;
At home, things jog along a railing,
Scarce moving, as if hobbled down.

I seem to hear a far-off droning,
Nightwatchmen's horn-sounds, dear and soft,
Nightwatchmen their refrains intoning,
And sobs of nightingales aloft.

Dem Dichter war so wohl daheime,
In Schildas teurem Eichenhain!
Dort wob ich meine zarten Reime
Aus Veilchenduft und Mondenschein.

In foolish Schilda's oaken grove
The poet's mood was so serene!
That's where my gauzy rhymes I wove
From violet scent and lunar sheen.

» Lebensfahrt

Ein Lachen und Singen! Es blitzen und gaukeln
Die Sonnenlichter. Die Wellen schaukeln
Den lustigen Kahn. Ich saß darin
Mit lieben Freunden und leichtem Sinn.

Der Kahn zerbrach in eitel Trümmer,
Die Freunde waren schlechte Schwimmer,
Sie gingen unter im Vaterland;
Mich warf der Sturm an den Seinestrand.

Ich hab' ein neues Schiff bestiegen,
Mit neuen Genossen; es wogen und wiegen
Die fremden Fluten mich hin und her—
Wie schwer mein Herz! Die Heimat wie fern!

Und das ist wieder ein Singen und Lachen—
Es pfeift der Wind, die Planken krachen—
Am Himmel erlischt der letzte Stern—
Mein Herz wie schwer! Die Heimat wie fern!

» Life's Journey

Laughter and song! The sun on the swells
Flashes and dances. The flood propels
The merry vessel; I took my part
With dear companions and carefree heart.

The barque broke up into planks and kindling;
The friends were not adept at swimming,
And they went down in the native land;
I was flung by the storm to the Seine's strand.

On another ship I embarked once more,
With new mates, off an alien shore;
I am rocked and cradled to and fro—
My home how far! My spirit how low!

And here again are songs and pranks—
A gale blows up to crack the planks;
Aloft there fades the final star—
How sad my heart! My home how far!

»   Ade, du heitres Franzosenvolk,
Ihr meine lustigen Brüder,
Gar närrische Sehnsucht treibt mich fort,
Doch komm ich in Kurzem wieder.

Denkt euch, mit Schmerzen sehne ich mich
Nach Torfgeruch, nach den lieben
Heidschnucken der Lüneburger Heid,
Nach Sauerkraut und Rüben.

Ich sehne mich nach Tabaksqualm,
Hofräten und Nachwächtern,
Nach Plattdeutsch, Schwarzbrot, Grobheit sogar,
Nach blonden Predigerstöchtern.

Auch nach der Mutter sehne ich mich,
Ich will es offen gestehen,
Seit dreiszehn Jahren hab ich nicht
Die alte Frau gesehen.

Ade, mein Weib, mein schönes Weib,
Du kannst meine Qual nicht fassen,
Ich drücke dich so fest an mein Herz,
Und muß dich doch verlassen.

Die lechzende Qual, sie treibt mich fort
Von meinem süßesten Glücke—
Muß wieder atmen deutsche Luft,
Damit ich nicht ersticke.

» Farewell, you cheerful folk of France,
My brethren's merry throng,
A foolish nostalgia drives me hence,
I'll be back, though, before long.

Imagine—I yearn beyond belief
For the smell of heather and peat,
For the dear toy sheep of the Lüneburg heath,
For pickled cabbage and beet.

I find I miss tobacco fug,
Black bread, the Low-German cadence,
The knighted, the night-watchmen—why, the boors!
The flaxen-haired parsonage maidens.

And also I am hankering,
Let me confess, for Mother;
I haven't seen the dear old thing
For thirteen years together.

Farewell, my wife, my lovely wife,
You can't fathom my distress;
I press you so fimly to my heart
But must leave you nonetheless.

I am driven away by that panting pain
From my sweetest happiness—
I must breathe German air again
Or draw no other breath.

Variae

Verschiedene

(1832–39)

》   Sie floh vor mir wie 'n Reh so scheu,
      Und wie ein Reh geschwinde!
      Sie kletterte von Klipp' zu Klipp',
      Ihr Haar das flog im Winde.

      Wo sich zum Meer der Felsen senkt,
      Da hab ich sie erreichet,
      Da hab ich sanft mit sanftem Wort
      Ihr sprödes Herz erweichet.

      Hier saßen wir so himmelhoch,
      Und auch so himmelselig;
      Tief unter uns, ins dunkle Meer
      Die Sonne sank allmählig.

      Tief unter uns, ins dunkle Meer,
      Versank die schöne Sonne;
      Die Wogen rauschten drüber hin,
      Mit ungestümer Wonne.

      O weine nicht, die Sonne liegt
      Nicht tot in jenen Fluten;
      Sie hat sich in mein Herz versteckt
      Mit allen ihren Gluten.

》   She fled from me like a timid deer,
Like a deer in startled unease;
She clambered down boulders and rock to rock,
Her tresses blown by the breeze.

Where cliffs plunge steeply down to the sea
At last I caught her apart,
And there I gently with soothing words
Softened her flinty heart.

And there we sat so heavenly high,
So heavenly bless'd sat we,
And far below us the westering sun
Met slowly the darkling sea.

The beautiful sun below us far
Sank in the shadowy sea,
And the waves went rushing over the place
In headlong ecstasy.

Oh, do not cry, the sun is not
Extinct in the surf's deep rivers;
He has taken refuge in my heart
With all his ardors and fevers.

» Schattenküsse, Schattenliebe,
Schattenleben, wunderbar!
Glaubst du, Närrin, alles bliebe
Unverändert, ewig wahr?

Was wir leiblich fest besessen
Schwindet hin wie Träumerein;
Und die Herzen, die vergessen,
Und die Augen schlafen ein.

» Shadow kisses, shadow bliss,
Shadow life, forever gay!
Do you think, dear foolishness,
Everything is here to stay?

What we lovingly possessed
Fades away like reverie;
Hearts grow heedless in the breast,
Eyes forget to see.

»   Das Fräulein stand am Meere
Und seufzte lang und bang,
Es rührte sie so sehre
Der Sonnenuntergang.

Mein Fräulein! sein Sie munter,
Das ist ein altes Stück;
Hier vorne geht sie unter
Und kehrt von hinten zurück.

» Young miss stood on the seashore,
By heavy sighs undone,
Moved to a rueful seizure
By the setting of the sun.

"Dear Miss, cheer up, look shoreward,
This is a well-worn turn;
The sun goes under forward
And comes back up astern."

» Wie schändlich du gehandelt,
Ich hab es den Menschen verhehlet,
Und bin hinausgefahren aufs Meer,
Und hab es den Fischen erzählet.

Ich laß dir den guten Namen
Nur auf dem festen Lande;
Aber im ganzen Ozean
Weiß man von deiner Schande.

》 I kept it a secret from people
How basely you dealt with me,
But I sailed far out on the ebbtide
And told the fish in the sea.

On terra firma I'll let you flaunt
A still unblemished name,
But everywhere on the ocean sea
They know about your shame.

» Es ragt ins Meer der Runenstein,
Da sitz ich mit meinen Träumen.
Es pfeift der Wind, die Möwen schrein,
Die Wellen, die wandern und schäumen.

Ich habe geliebt manch schönes Kind
Und manchen guten Gesellen.
Wo sind sie hin? Es pfeift der Wind,
Es schäumen und wandern die Wellen.

》 The runestone juts into the brine;
I sit beside it dreaming.
The seawinds hiss, the seagulls whine,
The surf, it goes foaming and streaming.

I have loved many a pretty miss
And some of the best lads roaming.
Where are they now? The seawinds hiss;
The surf, it goes streaming and foaming.

» Das Meer erstrahlt im Sonnenschein,
Als ob es golden wär.
Ihr Brüder, wenn ich sterbe,
Versenkt mich in das Meer.

Hab immer das Meer so lieb gehabt,
Es hat mit sanfter Flut
So oft mein Herz gekühlet;
Wir waren einander gut.

» The sun irradiates the sea
To golden jewelry;
You brothers, when I die,
Bury me in the sea.

I've always loved the ocean sea
With its caressing swell;
It has so often cooled my heart;
We wished each other well.

»   Wie rasch du auch vorüberschrittest,
Noch einmal schautest du zurück,
Der Mund, wie fragend, kühngeöffnet,
Stürmischer Hochmut in dem Blick.

O, daß ich nie zu fassen suchte
Das weiße flüchtige Gewand!
Die holde Spur der kleinen Füße,
O, daß ich nie sie wiederfand!

Verschwunden ist ja deine Wildheit,
Bist wie die Andern zahm und klar,
Und sanft und unerträglich gütig,
Und ach! nun liebst du mich sogar!

ANGELIQUE

» However swiftly you passed me first,
You still looked back in your advance,
Your lips, as if questioning, boldly pursed,
Fierce haughtiness in your glance.

Ah, that I never sought to grasp
Her fugitive raiment of white!
The charming tracks of her dainty feet,
That forever I lost their sight!

Gone is your wildness now; you are
Like the others, tame and clear of brow,
And mild, and insufferably kind;
And help! you even love me now!

》   Nimmer glaub ich, junge Schöne,
Was die spröde Lippe spricht;
Solche große schwarze Augen,
Solche hat die Tugend nicht.

Diese braungestreifte Lüge,
Streif sie ab; ich liebe dich.
Laß dein weißes Herz mich küssen—
Weißes Herz, verstehst du mich?

》 I won't credit, my young beauty,
What your fractious lip avers:
Such a pair of big black eyes are
Not the gems that virtue wears.

Come—this brown-and-white deception
Shed—my love is in your hand;
Let your heart-of-white caress me.
Heart-of-white—you understand?

»   Wenn ich, beseligt von schönen Küssen,
      In deinen Armen mich wohl befinde,
      Dann mußt du mir nie von Deutschland reden;
      Ich kanns nicht vertragen—es hat seine Gründe.

      Ich bitte dich, laß mich mit Deutschland in Frieden!
      Du mußt mich nicht plagen mit ewigen Fragen
      Nach Heimat, Sippschaft und Lebensverhältnis;
      Es hat seine Gründe—ich kanns nicht vertragen.

      Die Eichen sind grün, und blau sind die Augen
      Der deutschen Frauen, sie schmachten gelinde
      Und seufzen von Liebe, Hoffnung und Glauben;
      Ich kanns nicht vertragen—es hat seine Gründe.

》 When I feel blissful in your arms,
Carried away by kiss on kiss,
Don't talk of Germany to me,
I can't bear it—there are reasons for this.

I beg you, with Germany leave me in peace,
Don't plague me with questions, all hours and seasons,
Of homeland and kinsfolk and manner of living;
I cannot endure it—I have my reasons.

The oak trees are green, and blue are the eyes
Of German women; they languish a bit,
They whisper of love and of hope and of faith;
This I can't stand—there are reasons for it.

» Fürchte nichts, geliebte Seele,
Übersicher bist du hier;
Fürchte nicht, daß man uns stehle,
Ich verriegle schon die Tür.

Wie der Wind auch wütend wehe,
Er gefährdet nicht das Haus;
Daß auch nicht ein Brand entstehe,
Lösch ich unsre Lampe aus.

Ach, erlaube, daß ich winde
Meinen Arm um deinen Hals;
Man erkältet sich geschwinde
In Ermanglung eines Shawls.

》 Have no fear, beloved soul,
Here you're safe as safe can be;
Have no fear we might be stolen,
I have locked the door, you see?

Let the gale blow high and higher,
This firm house defies its might;
And against all risk of fire,
Here, let me snuff out our light.

Oh, just let my arm enfold
Your cool neck and shoulders all;
One so easily takes cold
When one doesn't wear a shawl.

»   Schaff mich nicht ab, wenn auch den Durst
Gelöscht der holde Trunk;
Behalt mich noch ein Vierteljahr,
Dann hab ich auch genung.

Kannst du nicht mehr Geliebte sein,
Sei Freundin mir sodann;
Hat man die Liebe durchgeliebt,
Fängt man die Freundschaft an.

» Do not dismiss me, even though
Quaffed is the heady brew;
Retain me yet three months or so,
Then I'll be ready too.

If you can't lover be, perforce
As friends we'll make a start,
When love has wholly run its course
Then friendship takes its part.

» Ehmals glaubt ich, alle Küsse,
Die ein Weib uns gibt und nimmt,
Seien uns, durch Schicksalsschlüsse,
Schon urzeitlich vorbestimmt.

Küsse nahm ich, und ich küßte
So mit Ernst in jener Zeit
Als ob ich erfüllen müßte
Taten der Notwendigkeit.

Jetzo weiß ich, überflüssig,
Wie so manches, ist der Kuß,
Und mit leichtern Sinnen küß ich
Glaubenlos im Überfluß.

》 Kisses (I was once persuaded)
Won from women or bestowed
Were all dealt those designated
Fatefully, ordained of old.

I shared kisses with my beauty
With such pious energy
As befits a sacred duty
Grounded in necessity.

Now I know they are redundant,
Like so much of all the rest,
And my kisses are abundant,
More lighthearted and unblessed.

»   Wir standen an der Straßeneck
Wohl über eine Stunde;
Wir sprachen voller Zärtlichkeit
Von unsrem Seelenbunde.

Wir sagten uns viel hundertmal,
Daß wir einander lieben;
Wir standen an der Straßeneck,
Und sind da stehn gelieben.

Die Göttin der Gelegenheit,
Wie'n Zöfchen, flink und heiter,
Kam sie vorbei und sah uns stehn,
Und lachend ging sie weiter.

》   There by the corner house we stood
       From two to well past three,
       Discussing in the tenderest terms
       Our souls' affinity.

       Times without number we avowed
       The love that we had found;
       There by the corner house we stood
       Like rooted to the ground.

       The muse of opportunity,
       Pert lady's maid and sprightly,
       In passing saw us standing there
       And sped on, laughing lightly.

» In meinen Tagesträumen,
In meinen nächtlichen Wachen,
Stets klingt mir in der Seele
Dein allerliebstes Lachen.

Denkst du noch Montmorencys,
Wie du auf dem Esel rittest,
Und von dem hohen Sattel
Hinab in die Disteln glittest?

Der Esel blieb ruhig stehen,
Fing an die Disteln zu fressen—
Dein allerliebstes Lachen
Werde ich nie vergessen.

》 Both in my daytime musing
And in wakeful nights thereafter,
My memory still rings
With your enchanting laughter.

Do you recall Montmorency,
When riding on an ass,
You slid from the tall saddle, straight
Into a thistly mass?

The donkey, calmly halting,
Began to feed at will—
Your sweet, contagious laughter
Is ever with me still.

»   Nicht lange täuschte mich das Glück,
Das du mir zugelogen,
Dein Bild ist wie ein falscher Traum
Mir durch das Herz gezogen.

Der Morgen kam, die Sonne schien,
Der Nebel ist zerronnen;
Geendigt hatten wir schon längst
Eh' wir noch kaum begonnen.

》   The bliss you conjured up for me
       Soon lost its spurious gleam,
       Your image drifted through my heart
       Like some mendacious dream.

       The morning dawned, the sun came out,
       Dispersed the mists you spun;
       We must have reached our end long since
       When we had scarce begun.

CLARISSE

»   Meinen schönsten Liebesantrag
Suchst du ängstlich zu verneinen;
Frag ich dann: ob das ein Korb sei?
Fängst du plötzlich an zu weinen.

Selten bet' ich, drum erhör mich,
Lieber Gott! Hilf dieser Dirne,
Trockne ihre süßen Tränen
Und erleuchte ihr Gehirne.

》   My most beautiful proposal
       You keep anxiously denying.
       When I ask, "Is this refusal?"
       Of a sudden you start crying.

       Seldom do I pray, so hear me,
       Lord, and help this charming jane;
       Dry her sweetly flowing tears
       And illuminate her brain.

» Überall wo du auch wandelst,
Schaust du mich zu allen Stunden,
Und je mehr du mich mißhandelst,
Treuer bleib ich dir verbunden.

Denn mich fesselt holde Bosheit,
Wie mich Güte stets vertrieben;
Willst du sicher meiner los sein,
Mußt du dich in mich verlieben.

》　Wheresoever you may walk,
You will see me, witness fond,
And the more you use me ill,
The more solid grows my bond.

Kindness always has repelled me,
Charming spite intrigued, you see;
To be rid of me for certain,
You must fall in love with me.

» Hol' der Teufel deine Mutter,
Hol' der Teufel deinen Vater,
Die so grausam mich verhindert,
Dich zu schauen im Theater.

Denn sie saßen da und gaben,
Breitgeputzt, nur seltne Lücken,
Dich im Hintergrund der Loge,
Süßes Liebchen, zu erblicken.

Und sie saßen da und schauten
Zweier Liebenden Verderben,
Und sie klatschten großen Beifall,
Als sie beide sahen sterben.

»   May the Devil take your mother,
       May your father catch the pox,
       Who malevolently blocked you
       From my sight in their gilt box.

       Broad-based there they sat, affording
       Scanty gaps where to divine
       Deep within the box an inkling
       Of your features, sweetheart mine.

       Planted there, they sat and watched
       The ruin of a loving pair
       And let loose a storm of clapping
       When they saw them perish there.

»   Geh nicht durch die böse Straße,
Wo die schönen Augen wohnen—
Ach! sie wollen allzugütig
Dich mit ihrem Blick verschonen.

Grüßen allerliebst herunter
Aus dem hohen Fensterbogen,
Lächeln freundlich (Tod und Teufel!),
Sind dir schwesterlich gewogen.

Doch du bist schon auf dem Wege,
Und vergeblich ist dein Ringen;
Eine ganze Brust voll Elend
Wirst du mit nach Hause bringen.

》   Don't go down the wicked street
        Where those eyes of beauty dwell,
        Sparing you their lightning flashes,
        Meaning oh so well;

        Where they wave delightful greetings
        From their lofty arch above,
        Smile so sweetly (hell, damnation!)
        With a sister's placid love.

        But you're on your way already,
        All your writhing is in vain,
        And you'll carry home with you
        A whole bellyful of pain.

»   Es kommt zu spät, was du mir lächelst,
Was du mir seufzest, kommt zu spät!
Längst sind gestorben die Gefühle,
Die du so grausam einst verschmäht.

Zu spät kommt deine Gegenliebe!
Es fallen auf mein Herz herab
All deine heißen Liebesblicke,
Wie Sonnenstrahlen auf ein Grab.

*

Nur wissen möcht ich: wenn wir sterben,
Wohin dann unsre Seele geht?
Wo ist das Feuer, das erloschen?
Wo ist der Wind, der schon verweht?

》 They come too late, those smiles you send me,
The sighs you launch are not returned!
Long, long extinct now are the feelings
That once so cruelly you spurned.

Too late, too late comes your requital,
And your impassioned gazes all
Descend upon my muted spirit
As sunbeams slant upon a pall.

*

I only wonder: when we die,
Just whither then our soul is bound?
Where is the fire when once extinguished?
Where may the bygone wind be found?

»   Diese Damen, sie verstehen,
Wie man Dichter ehren muß:
Gaben mir ein Mittagessen,
Mir und meinem Genius.

Ach! die Suppe war vortrefflich,
Und der Wein hat mich erquickt,
Das Geflügel, das war göttlich,
Und der Hase war gespickt.

Sprachen, glaub ich, von der Dichtkunst,
Und ich wurde endlich satt;
Und ich dankte für die Ehre,
Die man mir erwiesen hat.

》   Ah, these ladies know for certain
      How to treat a poet guest:
      Gave a festive four-course luncheon,
      For my genius, stewed and dressed.

      Ah, the soup was past comparing,
      And the wine refreshed my heart;
      And the poultry was transcendent,
      And the hare well laced with lard.

      There was talk of verse, I think;
      Then, fully dined and wined,
      I thanked them for the honor
      Conferred upon my mind.

» In welche soll ich mich verlieben,
Da beide liebenswürdig sind?
Ein schönes Weib ist noch die Mutter,
Die Tochter ist ein schönes Kind.

Die weißen, unerfahrnen Glieder,
Sie sind so rührend anzusehn!
Doch reizend sind geniale Augen,
Die unsre Zärtlichkeit verstehn.

Es gleicht mein Herz dem grauen Freunde,
Der zwischen zwei Gebündel Heu
Nachsinnlich grübelt, welch' von beiden
Das allerbeste Futter sei.

» Which should I fall in love with?
By both I am beguiled:
The mother's a beautiful woman still,
The daughter a beautiful child.

Those white and inexperienced limbs—
What dear delight to see!
How charming, though, congenial eyes
Responding tenderly.

My heart is like that famous ass
Between two equal bales of hay,
Who pondered which might be the best
His appetite to stay.

»   Die Flaschen sind leer, das Frühstück war gut,
Die Dämchen sind rosig erhitzet;
Sie lüften das Mieder mit Übermut,
Ich glaube sie sind bespitzet.

Die Schultern wie weiß, die Brüstchen wie nett!
Mein Herz erbebet vor Schrecken.
Nun werfen sie lachend sich aufs Bett,
Und hüllen sich ein mit den Decken.

Sie ziehen nun gar die Gardinen vor,
Und schnarchen am End um die Wette.
Da steh ich im Zimmer, ein einsamer Tor,
Betrachte verlegen das Bette.

》   The bottles are empty, the breakfast was good,
The flappers are flushed rose-pink;
From sheer high spirits they doff their stays,
I think they are tipsy with drink.

How white those shoulders, what dear little breasts!
My heart suspends its beats;
Now, laughing, they fling themselves on my bed
And wrap themselves in the sheets.

Here they are, drawing the curtains next,
Soon mingle their snores in profusion.
I stand in the room, alone and perplexed,
Eyeing my bed in confusion.

» Jugend, die mir täglich schwindet,
Wird durch raschen Mut ersetzt,
Und mein kühnrer Arm umwindet
Noch viel schlankre Hüften jetzt.

Tat auch manche sehr erschrocken,
Hat sie doch sich bald gefügt;
Holder Zorn, verschämtes Stocken,
Wird von Schmeichelei besiegt.

Doch, wenn ich den Sieg genieße,
Fehlt das Beste mir dabei.
Ist es die verschwundne, süße,
Blöde Jugendeselei?

» Losses which my aging faces
Are by ready nerve replaced:
Now my bolder arm embraces
Many more far slimmer waists.

Though some mimicked shock and trembling,
They quite soon gave in to me;
Charming anger, shy dissembling,
Overcome by flattery.

But as victory I savor,
What is more seems also less;
Do I miss that sweet lost flavor,
Adolescent oafishness?

»   Vierundzwanzig Stunden soll ich
Warten auf das höchste Glück,
Das mir blinzelnd süß verkündet,
Blinzelnd süß der Seitenblick.

O! die Sprache ist so dürftig,
Und das Wort ein plumpes Ding;
Wird es ausgesprochen, flattert
Fort der schöne Schmetterling.

Doch der Blick, der ist unendlich,
Und er macht unendlich weit
Deine Brust, wie einen Himmel
Voll gestirnter Seligkeit.

EMMA

》 Twice around the clock I'm bidden
Highest happiness to bide,
Which a sidelong wink has promised
Sweetly from a glance aside.

Language is a thing to pity,
And the word a lump of clay;
When it is pronounced, the pretty
Butterfly has flown away.

But a gaze can be unending,
For a glance can make your breast
Boundless, like a firmament
Full of starry happiness.

Far from Home

In der Fremde

» » »

Ich hatte einst ein schönes Vaterland.
Der Eichenbaum wuchs dort so hoch
Die Veilchen nickten sanft.
Es war ein Traum.

Das küßte mich auf deutsch und sprach auf deutsch
(Man glaubt es kaum, wie gut es klang)
Das Wort: "Ich liebe dich!"
Es war ein Traum.

》 》 》

I had a handsome homeland long ago.
The oak there grew so tall,
Meek violets curtsied low.
I dreamed it all.

In German I was kissed, in German heard
(Hard to believe how sweet they seemed)
The words "I love you" then!
It was all dreamed.

» Wo?

Wo wird einst des Wandermüden
Letzte Ruhestätte sein?
Unter Palmen in dem Süden?
Unter Linden an dem Rhein?

Werd' ich wo in einer Wüste
Eingescharrt von fremder Hand?
Oder ruh' ich an der Küste
Eines Meeres in dem Sand?

Immerhin! Mich wird umgeben
Gotteshimmel, dort wie hier,
Und als Totenlampen schweben
Nachts die Sterne über mir.

» Where?

Where is this way-weary rover's
Final resting-place to be?
Where the southern palm-frond hovers?
By a Rhenish linden tree?

Will I find in desert places
Shallow grave by alien hand?
Will I rest where sea-surf races,
Buried in a sandy strand?

There as here! Earth will be lustered
By the Lord's celestial light,
And as burial lamps, the clustered
Stars will shine on me at night.

Germany. A Winter's Tale

Deutschland. Ein Wintermärchen

(1844)

Ein neues Lied, ein besseres Lied,
O Freunde, will ich euch dichten!
Wir wollen hier auf Erden schon
Das Himmelreich errichten.

Wir wollen auf Erden glücklich sein,
Und wollen nicht mehr darben;
Verschlemmen soll nicht der faule Bauch
Was fleißige Hände erwarben.

Es wächst hienieden Brot genug
Für alle Menschenkinder,
Auch Rosen und Myrten, Schönheit und Lust,
Und Zuckererbsen nicht minder.

Ja, Zuckererbsen für jedermann,
Sobald die Schoten platzen!
Den Himmel überlassen wir
Den Engeln und den Spatzen.

A novel song, a better song,
My friends, I'll have you try!
Let's make a heaven here below,
Not wait for one in the sky.

We want to taste of bliss on earth,
No longer starve and wait,
Make greedy drones stop squandering
What toiling hands create.

This earth produces bread enough
For all who on it dwell,
And roses and myrtle, beauty and joy,
And sugarplums as well.

Yes—sugarplums for everyone
To sweeten bread and curds!
The kingdom of heaven we gladly leave
To the angels and the birds.

» Caput IX

Von Cöllen war ich drei Viertel auf Acht
Des Morgens fortgereiset;
Wir kamen nach Hagen schon gegen Drei,
Da wird zu Mittag gespeiset.

Der Tisch war gedeckt. Hier fand ich ganz
Die altgermanische Küche.
Sie mir gegrüßt, mein Sauerkraut,
Holdselig sind deine Gerüche!

Gestovte Kastanien im grünen Kohl!
So aß ich sie einst bei der Mutter!
Ihr heimischen Stockfische, seid mir gegrüßt!
Wie schwimmt ihr klug in der Butter!

Jedwedem fühlenden Herzen bleibt
Das Vaterland ewig teuer—
Ich liebe auch recht braun geschmort
Die Bücklinge und Eier.

Wie jauchzten die Würste im spritzelnden Fett!
Die Krammetsvögel, die frommen
Gebratenen Englein mit Apfelmus,
Sie zwitschern mir: "Willkommen!"

Willkommen, Landsmann,—zwitscherten sie—
Bist lange ausgeblieben,
Hast dich mit fremdem Gevögel so lang
In der Fremde herumgetrieben!

» Chapter IX

Having left Cologne at eight A.M.,
We came into Hagen station
Already at three in the afternoon
And stopped for a midday collation.

The table was set, and I found the fare
True German cuisine, to wit:
Dear sauerkraut, fermented with care:
Your fragrance is exquisite!

And chestnuts simmered in cabbage greens,
As Mum used to make with such savvy,
My native codfish, I dote on you!
How shrewdly you swim in your gravy!

Why, every truly sentient heart
Feels love of country and pride—
I too adore my kipper and eggs
Lovingly browned and fried.

Bratwursts exult as in grease they spatter!
The partridge thrush, those devout
Roasted putti with apple kraut,
"Be welcome home" they chatter.

They chirped to me: "Compatriot, hail!
But your constancy has been faulty;
How long you must have gadded about
With sundry foreign poultry!"

Es stand auf dem Tische eine Gans,
Ein stilles, gemütliches Wesen.
Sie hat vielleicht mich einst geliebt,
Als wir beide noch jung gewesen.

Sie blickte mich an so bedeutungsvoll,
So innig, so treu, so wehe!
Besaß eine schöne Seele gewiß,
Doch war das Fleisch zehr zähe.

Auch einen Schweinskopf trug man auf
In einer zinnernen Schüssel;
Noch immer schmückt man den Schweinen bei uns
Mit Lorbeerblättern den Rüssel.

There also was a roasted goose,
A sweet dumb bird sans feather;
She may have been in love with me once
When we were young together.

She looked at me with a gaze that spoke
Devotion, fervor, and woe!
She must have had a beautiful soul;
Her meat was leathery, though.

A pig's head, too, in a pewter mold
Was served on a bed of sorrel;
With us the swine still as of old
Get their muzzles wreathed in laurel.

» Caput XVI

Das Stoßen des Wagens weckte mich auf,
Doch sanken die Augenlider
Bald wieder zu, und ich entschlief
Und träumte vom Rotbart wieder.

Ging wieder schwatzend mit ihm herum
Durch alle die hallenden Säle;
Er frug mich dies, er frug mich das,
Verlangte, daß ich erzähle.

Er hatte aus der Oberwelt
Seit vielen, vielen Jahren,
Wohl seit dem Siebenjährigen Krieg,
Kein Sterbenswort erfahren.

Er frug nach Moses Mendelssohn,
Nach der Karschin, mit Intresse
Frug er nach der Gräfin Dubarry,
Des fünfzehnten Ludwigs Mätresse.

O Kaiser, rief ich, wie bist du zurück!
Der Moses ist längst gestorben,
Nebst seiner Rebekka, auch Abraham,
Der Sohn, ist gestorben, verdorben.

Der Abraham hatte mit Lea erzeugt
Ein Bübchen, Felix heißt er,
Der brachte es weit im Christentum,
Ist schon Kapellenmeister.

Chapter XVI

The jolts of the stagecoach woke me up,
But my eyelids rose in vain,
They presently drooped, and I fell asleep
And dreamt of the Redbeard again.

Chatting, I walked about with him
Through hall on echoing hall;
He asked me this, he asked me that,
Demanding I answer it all.

It seemed that from the upper world
For years he hadn't heard,
Perhaps as far back as the Seven Years' War,
Not a solitary word.

He asked about Moses Mendelssohn,
Mrs. Karsch, the poétesse,
He asked about Countess Dubarry,
Louis the Fifteenth's maîtresse.

"O Sire, that Moses is dead and gone,
How badly you're out of date!
Gone his Rebecca, and Abraham, too,
Their son, has met his fate.

"This Abraham fathered with Lea, his wife,
Young Felix, and he got on
Quite famously in the Gentile world,
Even wields an orchestral baton.

Die alte Karschin ist gleichfalls tot,
Auch die Tochter ist tot, die Klenke;
Helmine Chézy, die Enkelin,
Ist noch am Leben, ich denke.

Die Dubarry lebte lustig und flott,
Solange Ludwig regierte,
Der Fünfzehnte nämlich, sie war schon alt,
Als man sie guillotinierte.

Der König Ludwig der Fünfzehnte starb
Ganz ruhig in seinem Bette,
Der Sechzehnte aber ward guillotiniert
Mit der Königin Antoinette.

Die Königin zeigte großen Mut,
Ganz wie es sich gebührte,
Die Dubarry aber weinte und schrie,
Als man sie guillotinierte."——

Der Kaiser blieb plötzlich stille stehn,
Und sah mich an mit den stieren
Augen und sprach: "Um Gotteswilln,
Was ist das, guillotinieren?"

Das Guillotinieren—erklärte ich ihm—
Ist eine neue Methode,
Womit man die Leute jeglichen Stands
Vom Leben bringt zu Tode.

"Old lady Karsch is also gone,
And Klenke, the daughter, as well;
Her daughter, Chézy, is still alive,
As near as I can tell.

"La Dubarry led a gay old life
Throughout King Louis's reign,
Louis Quinze, that is; she was quite old
When she died on the guillotine.

"King Louis the Fifteenth, he died
Quite peacefully in his bed,
The Sixteenth, though, was guillotined
With his queen, Marie Antoinette.

"The Queen displayed great fortitude,
Did neither wince nor keen,
La Dubarry, though, screamed and boohooed
En route to the guillotine."

Abruptly the Emperor stopped in his track
And glared at me: "What is the meaning
Of what you keep saying, for heavens' sake
That sounds like 'guillotining'?"

"Why, guillotining"—I explained—
"Is a method, an innovation,
For speeding people from life to death,
Regardless of rank or station.

Bei dieser Methode bedient man sich
Auch einer neuen Maschine,
Die hat erfunden Herr Guillotin,
Drum nennt man sie Guillotine.

Du wirst hier an ein Brett geschnallt;—
Das senkt sich;—du wirst geschoben
Geschwinde zwischen zwei Pfosten;—es hängt
Ein dreieckig Beil ganz oben;—

Man zieht eine Schnur, dann schießt herab
Das Beil, ganz lustig und munter;—
Bei dieser Gelegenheit fällt dein Kopf
In einen Sack hinunter.

Der Kaiser fiel mir in die Red:
"Schweig still, von deiner Maschine
Will ich nichts wissen, Gott bewahr',
Daß ich mich ihrer bediene!

Der König und die Königin!
Geschnallt! an einem Brette!
Das ist ja gegen allen Respekt
Und alle Etikette!

Und du, wer bist du, daß du es wagst,
Mich so vertraulich zu duzen?
Warte, du Bürschchen, ich werde dir schon
Die kecken Flügel stutzen!

"This novel procedure, you must know,
Employs an advanced machine
Devised by a M. Guillotin,
So they call it a guillotine.

"They strap you first onto a board,
Then lower it by a lever,
Shove you between two posts, where on top
Is hung a triangular cleaver.

"A string is pulled, and the cleaver drops
With a merry whiz and crack;
On which occasion your headpiece hops
Into a waiting sack."

The Emperor interrupted me here:
"Stop! What a fiendish conception!
I'll hear no more, and God forbid
I should ever use this contraption!

"The King and his Consort! On a board!
Strapped down! The horrid impiety!
This flies in the face of all etiquette,
The height of impropriety!

"And you, who are you, brazen pup?
I've had enough of your lip;
Just wait, young sport, I am about
Your cheeky wings to clip!

Es regt mir die innerste Galle auf,
Wenn ich dich höre sprechen,
Dein Odem schon ist Hochverrat
Und Majestätsverbrechen!"

Als solchermaßen in Eifer geriet
Der Alte und sonder Schranken
Und Schonung mich anschnob, da platzen heraus
Auch mir die geheimsten Gedanken.

Herr Rotbart—rief ich laut—du bist
Ein altes Fabelwesen,
Geh, leg dich schlafen, wir werden uns
Auch ohne dich erlösen.

Die Republikaner lachen uns aus,
Sehn sie an unserer Spitze
So ein Gespenst mit Zepter und Kron';
Sie rissen schlechte Witze.

Auch deine Fahne gefällt mir nicht mehr,
Die altdeutschen Narren verdarben
Mir schon in der Burschenschaft die Lust
An den schwarzrotgoldnen Farben.

Das beste wäre, du bliebest zu Haus,
Hier in dem alten Kyffhäuser—
Bedenk ich die Sache ganz genau,
So brauchen wir gar keinen Kaiser.

"I'm ready to choke on my own bile
At what I have heard you say,
High treason is your very breath
And lèse majesté."

When the old fellow saw red and lost
Control and started to shout,
Barking at me so without restraint,
My innermost thoughts burst out.

"Sir Redbeard," I called out loud, "you are
A specter of legend and myth,
Go back to sleep, we'll free ourselves
Without you, better than with.

"Republicans will mock us to see
Stalking ahead of our rallies
A mummy like you with scepter and crown,
I can hear their tasteless sallies.

"Nor do I like your flag any more;
Since student fraternity weeks
The black, red, and gold has been spoilt for me
By those bonehead Germania freaks.

"You would do best to stay at home
Here in your old Kyffhäuser—
Giving the matter real thought, I find
We don't even need any kaiser."

Tragedy
Tragödie

» » »

Entflieh mit mir und sei mein Weib,
Und ruh an meinem Herzen aus;
Fern in der Fremde sei mein Herz
Dein Vaterland und Vaterhaus.

Gehst du nicht mit, so sterb ich hier
Und du bist einsam und allein;
Und bleibst du auch im Vaterhaus,
Wirst doch wie in der Fremde sein.

Elope with me and be my wife,
And use my heart to rest your head;
My heart will stand on alien shores
For homeland and in father's stead.

If you refuse to come, I'll die,
And you'll be lonely as if banned;
And though you stay in father's house,
You'll be in an alien land.

Romanzero

(1851)

» » »

Das Glück ist eine leichte Dirne
Und weilt nicht gern am selben Ort;
Sie streicht das Haar dir von der Stirne
Und küßt dich rasch und flattert fort.

Frau Unglück hat im Gegenteile
Dich liebefest ans Herz gedrückt;
Sie sagt, sie habe keine Eile,
Setzt sich zu dir ans Bett und strickt.

Good fortune is a flighty wench,
She wants no steady place to stay;
She'll stroke your hair, give it a wrench,
Blow you a kiss, and flit away.

Misfortune's hug is, *au contraire,*
A snug and matrimonial fit;
She's in no rush, she will declare,
Will settle by your bed, and knit . . .

» Jetzt Wohin?

Jetzt wohin? Der dumme Fuß
Will mich gern nach Deutschland tragen;
Doch es schüttelt klug das Haupt
Mein Verstand und scheint zu sagen:

Zwar beendigt ist der Krieg,
Doch die Kriegsgerichte blieben,
Und es heißt, du habest einst
Viel Erschießliches geschrieben.

Das ist wahr, unangenehm
Wär mir das Erschossenwerden;
Bin kein Held, es fehlen mir
Die pathetischen Gebärden.

Gern würd' ich nach England gehn,
Wären dort nicht Kohlendämpfe
Und Engländer—schon ihr Duft
Gibt Erbrechen mir und Krämpfe.

Manchmal kommt mir in den Sinn,
Nach Amerika zu segeln,
Nach dem grossen Freiheitstall,
Der bewohnt von Gleichheits-Flegeln—

Doch es ängstet mich ein Land,
Wo die Menschen Tabak käuen,
Wo sie ohne König kegeln,
Wo sie ohne Spucknapf speien.

» Whither Now?

Whither now? My foolish feet
Like to head for Germany;
But my reason shakes its head,
Seems to say sagaciously:

"Though the war is over now,
Martial law reigns as before,
And your pen has penned, they say,
Executables galore."

I'm no hero, and I'd find it
Quite unpleasant to be shot,
Lacking all the histrionics
So essential to that lot.

I would like to go to England,
Were it not for colliery damps
And the English—just their fragrance
Gives me nausea and cramps.

Now and then in thought I travel
To America, my sights
On that spacious freedom stable
Filled with louts of equal rights.

But I'm fearful of a land
Where the men are 'baccy chawers,
Where they bowl without a king,
And ignore the cuspidors.

Rußland, dieses schöne Reich,
Würde mir vielleicht behagen,
Doch im Winter könnte ich
Dort die Knute nicht ertragen.

Traurig schau' ich in die Höh',
Wo viel tausend Sterne nicken—
Aber meinen eignen Stern
Kann ich nirgends dort erblicken.

Hat im güldnen Labyrinth
Sich vielleicht verirrt am Himmel,
Wie ich selber mich verirrt
In dem irdischen Getümmel.

Russia, now, that handsome realm,
Might agree with me, who knows,
But I might not gladly bear
Being flogged in winter snows.

Woefully I gaze aloft,
Where a thousand starlets glitter
But my own good fortune's star
I find nowhere in that litter.

Haply it has gone astray
In those labyrinthine blazes,
Just as I have lost my way
Here in these terrestrial mazes.

» Weltlauf

Hat man viel, so wird man bald
Noch viel mehr dazubekommen;
Wer nur wenig hat, dem wird
Auch das wenige genommen.

Wenn du aber gar nichts hast,
Ach, so lasse dich begraben—
Denn ein Recht zum Leben, Lump,
Haben nur, die etwas haben.

» The Way of the World

He who earns a lot, to him
Much more still will soon accrue
He who little owns, from him
That will soon be taken too.

But if you own nothing, bum,
Let them speed you to your grave;
For the privilege to live, scum,
Nobody but owners have.

Posthumous

(1852–56)

» Lotosblume

Wahrhaftig, wir beide bilden
Ein kurioses Paar,
Die Liebste ist schwach auf den Beinen,
Der Liebhaber lahm sogar.

Sie ist ein leidendes Kätzchen,
Und er ist krank wie ein Hund,
Ich glaube, im Kopfe sind beide
Nicht sonderlich gesund.

Sie sei eine Lotosblume,
Bildet die Liebste sich ein;
Doch er, der blasse Geselle,
Vermeint der Mond zu sein.

Die Lotosblume erschließet
Ihr Kelchlein im Mondenlicht,
Doch statt befruchtenden Lebens
Empfängt sie nur ein Gedicht.

» Lotus Blossom

God knows, we two as a couple
Present a curious sight,
The lady has trouble walking;
Her lover limps outright.

She's like a suffering kitten,
He's sick as an ailing hound;
As far as heads go, neither
Would seem especially sound.

She is a lotus blossom,
The lady-love thinks in her heart;
He is the moon, so he fancies;
He's pale enough for the part.

The lotus flower is unfurling
By moonlight her little purse,
But in place of life-giving essence
All she gets to conceive is verse.

» Notes

"A single fir stands lonesome"   This poem has often been cited as an expression of Heine's longing for his "oriental," that is, Jewish identity, from which he had become separated. However, there is no clear index of this in the poem, and all attempts to claim Heine for any denomination or party should be regarded with skepticism.

"I see you in my dream each night"   *cypress*—In the classical tradition, the cypress is an emblem of death.

"Lorelei"   The Lorelei motif looks like a venerable legend, but was, in fact, a Romantic invention, only a few years old when Heine wrote this poem. The original word "Lureley" referred to the echo from the rock above the shoals in the Rhine at St. Goar. Its transformation into the name of a beautiful siren occurred in poems of 1802 by Clemens Brentano (1778–1842), of 1815 by Joseph von Eichendorff (1788–1857), and of 1821 by Count Otto von Loeben (1786–1825). All three poems are Christian parables. Heine's poem, written sometime in 1823, characteristically secularizes the motif.

"My heart, my heart is heavy"   *scarlet tunic*—The scene of this poem is Lüneburg, which belonged to the Kingdom of Hanover, at that time in personal union with the British crown. The sentry in the scarlet tunic is therefore a "redcoat," a soldier in British service. This is an example of the kind of political referent Heine smuggled into his love lyrics.

"We two, my dear, were children"   *children*—The poem was

originally addressed to Heine's sister, Charlotte Embden (1800–1899), to whom he was very attached. Having reached the age of almost a hundred years, she was the last living witness to Heine's whole life.

"Our hearts have concluded a pact"   *Holy Alliance*—The Holy Alliance was formed by Russia, Austria, and Prussia in 1815 after the defeat of Heine's hero Napoleon. Among its several forms of tyranny was the increasingly oppressive censorship under which Heine's generation of writers labored. Another example, obviously, of a barely coded political allusion.

"Heavens gray and workday-dismal!"   *Elbe River*—The Elbe is the river of Hamburg. Heine, who suffered repeated personal frustrations there and, in general, disliked all commercial centers, often adverted satirically and bitterly to the city. See also "Anno 1829."

"Anno 1829"   Lampooning the merchants of Hamburg. (Trans.)

"Anno 1839"   *Schilda's*—Schilda is the German version of the town of fools, like the Greek Abdera or the Jewish Chelm.

"Farewell, you cheerful folk of France"   These lines are from a manuscript variant to chapter 1 of *Germany. A Winter's Tale.*

"Both in my daytime musing"   *Montmorency*—A popular place for excursions north of Paris.

"Which should I fall in love with?"   *famous ass*—An allusion to the fable of "Buridan's Ass," in which an ass starves between two bundles of hay because he cannot choose between them.

"Where is this way-weary rover's" Pushkin's famous poem "As down the noisy streets I wander" (1829) ends as follows:

> And where, fate, is my death preparing?
> At sea, a-roving, in the fray?
> Or will this nearby vale be bearing
> Within its earth my feel-less clay?
>
> Although my flesh will be past caring
> About the site of its decay,
> Yet I would gladly still be sharing
> The dear haunts of my earthly day.
>
> And close to my sepulchral portals
> I want young life to be at play,
> And nature, unconcerned with morals,
> To shed its beauty's timeless ray. (Trans. W. W. A.)

(Trans.)

Germany. A Winter's Tale, Chapter XVI   *Redbeard*—Emperor Frederick I (ca. 1120–90), called Barbarossa, one of the most successful of the Holy Roman Emperors. In a legend originally applied to his grandson, Frederick II (1194–1250), the last German emperor before the Interregnum, but subsequently transferred to Barbarossa, he was supposed to be waiting, with his men and horses, in the Kyffhäuser Mountain in Thuringia for the moment of the restoration of German power and unity. In Heine's time the legend began what was to be a long-lived revival in the interest of German nationalism. *Seven Years' War*—A world war (1756–63) between France, Austria, Russia, Saxony, Sweden, and Spain on one side and Prussia, England,

and Hanover on the other. The American theater is known as the French and Indian War. *Moses Mendelssohn*—Moses Mendelssohn (1729–86), philosopher; the first Jew to become a prestigious figure in German intellectual life. *Mrs. Karsch*—Anna Luise Karsch (1722–91), commonly known as "die Karschin," a poet of extremely humble and abusive origins who earned the patronage of the literary world and the Prussian court. *Countess Dubarry*—Jeanne Bécu, Countess du Barry (1743–93), influential mistress of Louis XV. *Rebecca*—In order to maintain his biblical paradigm, Heine renames Fromet Mendelssohn, née Gugenheim (1737–1812), Moses Mendelssohn's wife. *Abraham*—Abraham Mendelssohn (1776–1835), one of Moses Mendelssohn's sons. *Lea*—Lea Mendelssohn, née Salomon (1777–1842), wife of Abraham Mendelssohn. *Felix*—Felix Mendelssohn-Bartholdy (1809–47), famous composer. At this time he was a protégé of the king of Prussia, Frederick William IV, who had put him in charge of church music and symphony concerts at the Berlin court. Heine took a dim view of these activities. *Gentile world*—Mendelssohn-Bartholdy's father Abraham was one of the four of Moses Mendelssohn's six children who converted to Christianity. *Klenke*—Karsch's daughter Karoline Luise von Klencke (1754–1802), playwright and poet. *Chézy*—Klencke's daughter Wilhelmine Christiane von Chézy (1783–1856), poet. *Guillotin*—Joseph-Ignace Guillotin (1738–1814), physician, did not invent the guillotine but advocated it as a humane, painless device for execution. *black, red, and gold*—Black, red, and gold were the colors of German liberalism and nationalism, at this time primarily a student movement. The colors were banned but constantly employed in subversive devices. Eventually they were to be associated with the democratic tradition and became the colors of the flag of the Federal Republic of Germany after World War II. *Germania freaks*—Germania was one of the German student fraternities, or *Burschenschaften,* that campaigned for a unified, constitutional German nation. At this time the fraternity was underground, having been banned by a law of 1819, which threatened its leaders with death. While no such sentence was ever carried out, some activists suffered long fortress prison terms. Whatever progressive impulses the movement may have had, it was viewed by Heine as hopelessly contaminated with German nationalism and reactionary Romanticism, which he abhorred as repressive, religious, anti-Semitic, and hostile to France.

"Whither Now?"   *war is over now*—The poem appears to have been written shortly after the revolution of March 1848, during which the censorship regulations, which Heine and his publisher, with twenty years of immense effort, had fought to something like a draw, collapsed in one German state after another. Heine, however, thought that the thaw might not be reliable, and in this he was prescient. *king*—The pun is a little difficult to capture. In the German game of ninepins, the larger, center pin is called the "king" (similar to the original meaning of our "kingpin"). Heine repeatedly declared that he was a monarchist. *flogged*—The original playfully puts *Knute* (knout) here instead of the expected *Kälte;* hence "winter-flogged" for "winter-logged." (Trans.)

"The Way of the World"   *be taken too*—Cf. Luke 19:26: "For I say unto you, that unto every one which hath shall be given; and from him that hath not, even that he hath shall be taken away from him." Belligerent glosses on biblical texts are particularly frequent in the late poetry, after Heine's announced return to God.